Beginners' Brazilian Portuguese

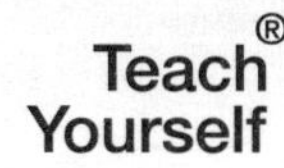

Beginners' Brazilian Portuguese

Sue Tyson-Ward
and Ethel Pereira de Almeida Rowbotham

First published in Great Britain in 2015 as *Get Started in Brazilian Portuguese* by Hodder and Stoughton. An Hachette UK company.

This edition published by Teach Yourself in 2025
An imprint of John Murray Press

1

Editorial support from Haremi Ltd

Revised artworks © Nadene Naude (Beehive Illustration)

Photographs © Shutterstock.com

A CIP catalogue record for this title is available from the British Library

Paperback ISBN 978 1 399 82173 5
ebook ISBN 978 1 399 82174 2

Typeset by Integra Software Services Pvt. Ltd., Pondicherry, India

Printed and bound in Great Britain by Clays Ltd, Elcograf S.p.A.

John Murray Press policy is to use papers that are natural, renewable and recyclable products and made from wood grown in sustainable forests. The logging and manufacturing processes are expected to conform to the environmental regulations of the country of origin.

John Murray Press
Carmelite House
50 Victoria Embankment
London EC4Y 0DZ

Teach Yourself
John Murray Press
123 S. Broad St., Ste 2750
Philadelphia, PA 19109

www.teachyourself.com

The authorised representative in the EEA is Hachette Ireland, 8 Castlecourt Centre, Dublin 15, D15 XTP3, Ireland (email: info@hbgi.ie)

John Murray Press, part of Hodder & Stoughton Limited
An Hachette UK company

Contents

About the authors

Sue Tyson-Ward has had a connection with Portuguese since living with a Portuguese family prior to starting her studies at Oxford in 1984. During her degree course she spent a year in Brazil, an experience which she has drawn on frequently over the years in her teaching and writing. Since graduating with a degree in Portuguese and Spanish in 1988, she has lived, worked and studied in Portugal, and has also been back to Brazil.

Sue has written a number of books on Portuguese and Brazilian language, life and culture. She was invited to act as language consultant for the BBC's highly acclaimed TV series *Talk Portuguese*, and also gave initial advice for the *Brazil Inside Out* series.

She has been involved in Portuguese examinations in the UK since 1992, including roles as Moderator for GCSE speaking tests, Principal Examiner for GCSE Writing and Principal Moderator for Asset Speaking tests; she was also the Subject Officer for Portuguese at the Awarding Body. She continues to act as a Vetter for International Examinations in Portuguese.

Sue teaches the language and culture in Lancaster, and prepares research students at the university for a variety of field trips to Brazil. She is a keen and enthusiastic promoter of all things relating to the Portuguese-speaking world.

Ethel Pereira de Almeida Rowbotham was born in Rio de Janeiro, moving later to Brasília, where she studied Politics and International Relations before moving to the UK. She taught Portuguese at all levels in the UK for more than 25 years, and has worked at the University of Central Lancashire, Bolton Community College and Lancashire College. She also worked as an interpreter and translator and was a GCSE reviser.

About the course

The aim of this course is to enable learners, with no previous knowledge of the language, to speak and understand Brazilian Portuguese and to go beyond basic, survival level, be it for leisure, business or family reasons.

In Brazil, most people do not speak English fluently. If you venture away from the major touristic cities or resorts you will definitely need to speak some Portuguese. Taxi drivers and staff at bus stations and shops will most likely speak very little or no English at all.

There are more than 230 million Portuguese speakers in the world and of those, 213 million are Brazilians. Brazilian Portuguese is the dominant form of Portuguese on social media, programs on TV and streaming platforms, and music in the Portuguese speaking world.

Brazilians are masters in adding new vocabulary to the language! New words and expressions tend to start in Brazil and then pervade other Portuguese speaking countries through television, books and social media. Soon the new words start appearing in the official dictionary.

If you learn Brazilian Portuguese, you will be able to visit any Portuguese-speaking country and you will be understood by the locals, even if you find it a bit difficult to understand their particular accent!

Treat this journey of learning as an adventure and start planning your trip to Brazil while you grow your vocabulary and improve your pronunciation.

How to use this book

A little goes a long way!

Try to use the book little and often, rather than for long stretches at a time. This will help you to create a study habit, much in the same way you would learn a sport or music. Leave the book somewhere handy so that you can pick it up for just a few minutes to refresh your memory.

Before you start, make a plan!

Setting goals affects the programming of your brain, strengthening neural pathways and ultimately making it more likely that you will achieve those goals. Before you begin, think about how much time you want to devote to learning, which skills or areas you want to focus on, and identify specific ideas you want to be able to communicate or activities you want to engage in.

Track your progress!

Start a notebook to use for study, where you can create vocabulary lists, a grammar summary, questions you'd like answered, etc. Keep track of your resources – write down the names of films, podcasts, songs or blogs you like, and jot down a few words or expressions you may have recognized or learned. The more you can reflect on your learning process, the deeper your connection with the language will be. If you need more guidance in this process, we recommend Teach Yourself *Fluentish: Language Learning Planner & Journal* by Jo Franco.

Use the tools at the beginning of each unit to help you set goals, plan your time, and keep track of the work you do.

IN THIS UNIT, YOU WILL LEARN HOW TO

Each unit begins with an overview of the language you will be learning and skills you will be acquiring.

MY PROGRESS TRACKER

Use the progress tracker to plan your study time and to keep a record of what you've accomplished. The first column tracks time, and the remaining five columns represent the skills you'll be working on: listening, pronunciation, reading, writing, and spoken interaction.

Personalize the tracker: Instead of the date or day, you can enter an increment of time (15 minutes, 1 hour ...). Add columns for culture, vocabulary, grammar or any other area you wish to focus on. Give yourself a star when you feel you've done particularly well. Make it your own! Review your tracker regularly and see which areas could use more practice.

Use the **Self check** at the end of each unit to evaluate your progress.

Try to practice each skill every day.

The icons in the progress tracker are used throughout the book to help you easily identify and locate the skills you want to practice:

 Listening skills

 Speaking – pronunciation skills

 Reading skills

 Writing skills

 Speaking – conversation skills

Remember: there are many ways to build your skills in addition to those provided in this book: use a language-learning app, listen to music or podcasts, watch TV shows or movies, go to a restaurant, follow social media accounts in Brazilian Portuguese, read blogs, newspapers or magazines, switch the language settings in your apps, or sign up for a language exchange or a tutor.

Each unit in *Beginners' Brazilian Portuguese* is structured in the following way:

What you will learn identifies what you should be able to do in Portuguese by the end of the unit.

Culture points present cultural aspects related to the themes in the units, introducing key words and phrases and including follow-up questions.

Vocabulary builder introduces key unit vocabulary grouped by theme and conversation, accompanied by audio. By learning the words and listening to them, your progress in learning contemporary Brazilian Portuguese will be swift.

New expressions introduces the key expressions you will hear in the conversations. Listen to them on the audio and look at how they are expressed as these will aid your comprehension of the conversations. You will have the opportunity to use some of the expressions yourself in exercises and activities.

Conversations are recorded dialogues that you can listen to and practice, beginning with a narrative that helps you understand what you are going to hear, with a focusing question and follow-up activities.

Language discovery draws your attention to key language points in the conversations and to rules of grammar. Read the notes and look at the conversations to see how the language is used in practice.

Practice offers a variety of exercises, including speaking opportunities, to give you a chance to see and use words and phrases in their context.

Speaking and listening offer practice in speaking and understanding Portuguese through exercises that let you use what you have learned in previous units.

Reading and writing provide practice in reading everyday items and contain mostly vocabulary from the unit. Try to get the main point of the text before you answer the follow-up questions.

Pronunciation gives you another opportunity to focus on a particular tricky sound in Brazilian Portuguese, by listening to some words and imitating the speaker.

Language tip boxes aim to give you extra snippets of vocabulary, cultural tips or helpful pointers for remembering specific expressions.

Test yourself helps you assess what you have learned. You learn more by doing the tests without consulting the text, and only when you have done them check if your answers are the correct ones (do not cheat!).

Self-check lets you see what you can do after having completed each unit.

Review units sum up what you have learned in the previous units. There are three review units: after Unit 3, after Unit 6 and after Unit 10. If you master all the questions in the review unit, go ahead with the next unit; if not, go back and refresh your knowledge.

The **Answer key** helps you check your progress by including answers to the activities both in the text units and the review units.

Once you have completed all ten units in this book successfully, you may want to proceed with more advanced Brazilian Portuguese course books, such as *Teach Yourself Complete Brazilian Portuguese*. Bilingual dictionaries and Portuguese grammars, such as the *Teach Yourself Essential Portuguese Grammar*, will be of much use. There are many internet resources for learning Portuguese, including sites for popular Brazilian journals, magazines, TV and radio stations, and YouTube channels.

Learn to learn

The Discovery method

This book incorporates the Discovery method of learning. You will be encouraged throughout the course to engage your mind and figure out the meaning for yourself, through identifying patterns and understanding grammatical concepts, noticing words that are similar to English, and more. As a result of your efforts, you will be able to retain what you have learned, use it with confidence and continue to learn the language on your own after you have finished this book.

Everyone can succeed in learning a language – the key is to know how to learn it. Learning is more than just reading or memorizing grammar and vocabulary. It is about being an active learner, learning in real contexts and using what you have learned in different situations. If you figure something out for yourself, you are more likely to understand it, and when you use what you have learned, you are more likely to remember it.

As many of the essential details, such as grammar rules, are introduced through the Discovery method, you will have more fun while learning. The language will soon start to make sense and you will be relying on your own intuition to construct original sentences independently, not just by listening and repeating.

Happy learning!

Be successful at learning languages

There are many strategies that can help you become a successful language learner. Different people have different learning styles and some of these approaches will be more effective for you than others. Use this list as a point of inspiration when you want to find the most effective ways to advance your skills and begin your journey to fluency.

VOCABULARY

- To organize your study of vocabulary, group new words under:
  - **a** generic categories, e.g. *food, furniture*.
  - **b** situations in which they occur, e.g. under *restaurant* you can write *server, table, menu, bill*.

c functions, e.g. greetings, parting, thanks, apologizing.

- Say the words out loud as you read them.
- Write the words over and over again. Remember that if you want to keep lists on your phone or tablet you can usually switch the keyboard language to make sure you are able to include all accents and special characters.
- Listen to the audio several times.
- Cover up the English side of the vocabulary list and see if you remember the meaning of the word.
- Associate the words with similar sounding words in English, e.g. **estudar** (*to study*) with the action of studying, **banco** with *bank*.
- Create flash cards, drawings and mind maps.
- Write words for objects around your house and stick them to the objects.
- Pay attention to patterns in words, e.g. adding **bom** or **boa** to the start of a phrase can often indicate a greeting, **bom dia**, **boa tarde**, **boa noite**.
- Experiment with words. Use the words that you learn in new contexts and find out if they are correct. For example, you learn in Unit 2 that **ter** means *to have*, e.g. **tenho dois filhos** (*I have two children / sons*), and is also used to say how old you are: **tenho 25 anos** (*I am 25 years old*). Experiment with **tenho** in new contexts, e.g. **tenho uma casa bonita** (*I have a pretty house*), **tenho um carro azul** (*I have a blue car*). Check the new phrases either in this book, in a dictionary or with Brazilian Portuguese speakers.

GRAMMAR

- To organize the study of grammar write your own grammar glossary and add new information and examples as you go along.
- Experiment with grammar rules.
- Sit back and reflect on the rules you learn. See how they compare with your own language or other languages you may already speak. Try to find out some rules on your own and be ready to spot the exceptions. By doing this you'll remember the rules better and get a feel for the language.
- Try to find examples of grammar in conversations or other articles.
- Keep a 'pattern bank' that organizes examples that can be listed under the structures you've learned.
- Use old vocabulary to practice new grammar structures.
- When you learn a new verb form, write the conjugation of several different verbs you know that follow the same form.

PRONUNCIATION

- When organizing the study of pronunciation keep a section of your notebook for pronunciation rules and practice those that trouble you.
- Repeat all of the conversations, line by line. Listen to yourself and try to mimic what you hear.
- Record yourself and compare yourself to a Brazilian Portuguese speaker.
- Make a list of words that give you trouble and practice them.
- Study individual sounds, then full words.
- Don't forget, it's not just about pronouncing letters and words correctly, but also using the right intonation. So, when practicing words and sentences, mimic the rising and falling intonation of Brazilian Portuguese speakers.

LISTENING AND READING

The conversations in this book include questions to help guide you in your understanding. But you can go further by following some of these tips.

- **Imagine the situation.** When listening to or reading the conversations, try to imagine where the scene is taking place and who the main characters are. Let your experience of the world help you guess the meaning of the conversation, e.g. if a conversation takes place in a restaurant you can predict the kind of vocabulary that is being used.
- **Concentrate on the main part.** When watching a film in another language you usually get the meaning of the whole story from a few individual shots. Understanding a conversation or article is similar. Concentrate on the main parts to get the message and don't worry about individual words.
- **Guess the key words**; if you cannot, ask or look them up.
- When there are key words you don't understand, try to guess what they mean from the context. If you're listening to a Brazilian Portuguese speaker and cannot get the gist of a whole passage because of one word or phrase, try to repeat that word with a questioning tone; the speaker will probably paraphrase it, giving you the chance to understand it. If for example you wanted to find out the meaning of the word **molho** (*sauce*), you would ask **O que quer dizer molho?** or **O que é molho?**

WRITING

You'll have plenty of writing practice using this book. Creating vocabulary lists, grammar summaries and taking good notes as you study is another great opportunity to practice writing.

If you're keeping your lists or notes on your smartphone, computer or tablet, remember to switch the keyboard language to be able to include all accents and special characters. Here are some other ways to practice writing:

- Write out the answers to all Practice and Test Yourself questions.
- Create your own vocabulary lists and a grammar summary.
- Look up writing prompts for language learning or try writing a daily gratitude journal in Brazilian Portuguese.
- Write out your To Do and shopping lists in Brazilian Portuguese.
- Join online forums and discussion groups about or in Brazilian Portugese.

SPEAKING

Rehearse in the language you are learning. As all language teachers will assure you, the successful learners are those students who overcome their inhibitions and get into situations where they must speak, write and listen to the language. Here are some useful tips to help you practice speaking Brazilian Portuguese:

- Hold a conversation with yourself, using the conversations of the units as models and the structures you have learned previously.
- After you have conducted a transaction with a sales assistant or server in your own language, pretend that you have to do it in Brazilian Portuguese.
- Look at objects around you and try to name them in Brazilian Portuguese.
- Look at people around you and try to describe them in detail.
- Try to answer all of the questions in the book out loud.
- Say the dialogues out loud then try to replace sentences with ones that are true for you.
- Try to role play different situations in the book.

Learn from your errors

- Don't let errors interfere with getting your message across. Making errors is part of any normal learning process, but some people get so worried that they won't say anything unless they are sure it is correct. This leads to a vicious circle as the less they say, the less practice they get and the more mistakes they make.
- Note the seriousness of errors. Many errors are not serious as they do not affect the meaning; for example if you use the wrong article (**o** for **a**) or the wrong pronouns (**ela fala** for **ele fala**). So concentrate on getting your message across and learn from your mistakes.

Learn to cope with uncertainty

- Don't over-use your dictionary. When reading a text in the language you're learning don't be tempted to look up every word you don't know. Underline the words you do not understand and read the passage several times, concentrating on trying to get the gist of the passage. If after the third time there are still words which prevent you from getting the general meaning of the passage, look them up in the dictionary.
- Don't panic if you don't understand.
- If at some point you feel you don't understand what you are told, don't panic or give up listening. Either try and guess what is being said and keep following the conversation or, if you cannot, isolate the expression or words you haven't understood and have them explained to you. The speaker might paraphrase them and the conversation will carry on.
- Keep talking.
- The best way to improve your fluency in a language is to talk every time you have the opportunity to do so: keep the conversations flowing and don't worry about the mistakes. If you get stuck for a particular word, don't let the conversation stop; paraphrase or replace the unknown word with one you do know, even if you have to simplify what you want to say.

Brazilian Portuguese

Although Brazilian Portuguese is a 'variant' of the Portuguese language, just as that spoken in Portugal itself is, Brazilian speakers manage to make their language sound as laid-back as they are themselves. It is actually easier to understand a Brazilian speaker than a speaker of European Portuguese, as Brazilians tend to open their vowels more, so you can hear more of the words, and they often sound as though they are 'samba-ing' round the language. Studded with all kinds of mannerisms and gestures, conversation with Brazilian speakers is interesting, often fun, but sometimes needs time to work round some of the common speech habits. A typical example, often difficult to decipher for someone listening in, is the contraction of the word **está** (*is / are*) to just **tá**. So, you may hear **tá legal!** (*that's great!*) – **legal** being one of those words used by every Brazilian speaker to mean something is *great*, *super*, *wicked*, etc. Other such colourful expressions include: **beleza!** or **que beleza!** (*how fantastic!*), **ótimo** (*brilliant*), **tô (estou) nem aí** (*I'm not bothered*), **nossa!** (*wow!*), and **vij / vixe** (short for **Virgem Maria** – a more benign way of expressing 'God'-type phrases of amazement). Whoops of excitement are conveyed through **opa!** and **oba!**; anything in a mess or shambles is a **bagunça**.

If you have had any previous exposure to the Portuguese spoken in Portugal, you will notice a few differences between that and Brazilian Portuguese, the main ones being the pronunciation of certain sounds and vocabulary. So, whereas in Portugal **boa noite** (*good evening*) is pronounced 'boh-uh noy-t', in Brazil you are more likely to hear 'boh-a noy-chee', the '-te' sound in Brazil being a distinctive '-chee'. In a similar way, the '-de' sound differs: the word for *city* (**cidade**) is usually 'see-da-duh' in Portugal, but 'see-da-dgee' in Brazil. There are slight regional variations, but on the whole the '-te' and '-de' sounds of Brazil are very easy to listen out for. In terms of vocabulary, in the same way as British and American English uses different words, so too do Brazilian and European Portuguese, sometimes to a confusing extent. A *train* is **comboio** in Portugal but **trem** in Brazil; *breakfast* in Portugal is **pequeno almoço** but **café da manhã** in Brazil. Some grammatical structures are also slightly different. Speakers from Portugal, for example, will say **Chamo-me Clara** (*I am called*

Clara), whereas a Brazilian speaker would say **Eu me chamo X**; Brazilian speakers call most people **Você** (*you*), but in Portugal there is a minefield of forms of address. Brazilian speakers also incorporate many English words into their everyday speech, sometimes giving them their slant on pronunciation; the words **shopping** (*shopping centre*) and **short** (*shorts*) are commonplace.

Given the size of Brazil, Brazilian Portuguese has much more consistency as a language than many expect. Although not a lot of data exists as yet on the variations within Brazil, the main differences appear to be based on pronunciation, especially the vowel sounds. Some research to date has attempted to categorize a 'northern' and 'southern' group of variants. Some of the more distinct Brazilian Portuguese accents include carioca, which is spoken in the state and city of Rio de Janeiro. In Rio Grande do Sul, the **gaúcho** accent is quite distinct. There are also different accents in the northern states of Ceará and Bahia. Of course, once you venture into the Amazon areas, you will encounter indigenous languages spoken by many indigenous tribes.

MAP OF BRAZIL

Pronunciation guide

Here is a simple guide to the letters of the alphabet, their Brazilian Portuguese name (in square brackets) and how to pronounce them.

The Portuguese alphabet is the same as the Roman one used in English and other Latin-based languages. Although the letters K, W and Y do not appear in Brazilian Portuguese words, the letters exist for use in words from other languages and abbreviations, and under the new spelling agreement (see below) have been incorporated into the alphabet proper.

00.01 **Listen to the whole alphabet on the audio a few times, then try to join in.**

A [a] ah	**B** [bê] bay	**C** [cê] say	**D** [dê] day	**E** [é] eh	**F** [efe] eh-fee
G [gê] zhay	**H** [agá] ah-gah	**I** [i] ee	**J** [jota] zhoh-tah	**K** [ka] ka	**L** [ele] eh-lee
M [eme] eh-mee	**N** [ene] eh-nee	**O** [ó] oh	**P** [pê] pay	**Q** [quê] kay	**R** [erre] air-hee
S [esse] eh-ssee	**T** [tê] tay	**U** [u] oo	**V** [vê] vay	**W** [dáblio] dabble-yoo	**X** [xis] shish
Y [ípsilon] ip-see-lon	**Z** [zê] zay				

Most Portuguese words are pronounced as they are written – there are far fewer 'hidden' sounds or awkward sounds than in some other languages, such as English or French. However, when Brazilians speak, they often add a vowel, usually a **y** (ee) in words that end in some consonants (mainly **d**, **k**, **t**) such as:

Facebook (Facybooky)

Internet (Internetchy)

Ford (Forjy)

Fiat (Fiatchy)

Hot dog (hotchy doggy)

Names of people: *Mark (Marky)*, *David (Davijy)*, *Nick (Nicky)*

Portuguese also has its own version of many English words, such as:

picnic (**piquenique**)

whisky (**uísque**)

New York (**Nova Iorque**)

Once you have decoded a few tricky sounds, you should be able to have a go at reading Portuguese out loud as you see it. The following are some basic guidelines for some of the less straightforward pronunciations:

Portuguese letter(s)	Pronunciation
ch	*sh*
lh	like the *lli* in *million*
nh	like the *ni* in *onion*
g, followed by **e / i**	like the *s* in *pleasure*
j	as above
h	always silent
x	tricky – varies from a hard *ks* sound to a *z*, or even *sh*

Nasal sounds pronounced at the back of the nose are indicated by a **~** over the vowel, and also include words ending in **-m** or **-n**. Try to imagine saying them with a bad cold, when your nose is slightly blocked!

ão	*ow*
ãos	*ows*
õe	*oy*
ões	*oys*
ã	*ah*
ãs	*ahs*
ãe	*eye*
ães	*eyes*

One thing to remember is that when words run together when spoken, there is an effect on the ending and beginning of words involved, which may alter the sound from when a word is spoken in isolation from others.

A quick note here about the consonants **c**, **g** and **q**, which change their pronunciation depending on which vowels follow them. This can be a stumbling block for the uninitiated, hence a basic rule here:

c before **a**, **o** or **u** = hard sound, like *cat*

ç before **a**, **o** or **u** = soft sound, like *face*

c before **e** or **i** = soft sound

g before **e** or **i** = soft sound, like the *s* sound in *treasure*

g before **a**, **o** or **u** = hard sound, like in *goal*

g + **u** before **e** or **i** = 'silent' **u**, e.g. **guitarra** (*guitar*) = *ghee* ... NOT *gwee* ... There are some exceptions (there always are!), such as **linguiça** (*spicy sausage*) = *lingwiça*.

q is always followed by **u**

qu before **e** or **i** = 'silent' **u**, e.g., **máquina** *(machine) mákeena*, NOT *mákweena;* again, there are some exceptions – make a note of them when you learn them.

qu before **o** or **a** = *kw*, e.g. **quadro** (*picture*) = *kwadro*

ph does not exist in Portuguese: those words similar to English are spelled with an **f** – the sound is the same, but be careful with the spelling: e.g. **filósofo** (*philosopher*).

You will have the opportunity throughout the ten units of this course to focus on how to pronounce some of the trickier sounds. By listening carefully to the Brazilian Portuguese speaker, and trying to imitate how they say the words, you will improve your spoken Portuguese enormously!

Brazilian spelling

After many years of wrangling over spelling throughout the Portuguese-speaking world (and most particularly between Portugal and Brazil), up-to-date orthographic (spelling) agreements have been implemented under the new **Acordo Ortográfico**. However, there are still some differences in spelling between the two main variants of the language, Brazilian and Luso-African, which includes those African countries with Portuguese as an official language. If you have studied European Portuguese before now, you will notice slight differences in spelling, for example: EP **rececionista** / BP **recepcionista** (*receptionist*).

Accents

You will find the following written accents in Portuguese:

´	*acute accent*	**acento agudo**	opens vowel sound and indicates stress*	**cardápio** (*menu*)
^	*circumflex*	**circunflexo**	closes vowel sound and indicates stress	**inglês** (*English*)
~	*tilde*	**til**	nasalizes vowel and usually indicates stress	**estação** (*station*)

`	*grave accent*	**acento grave**	opens vowel, non-stressing, indicates a contraction of two words	**àquela** = **a** + **aquela** (*to that*)

* Stress is when you emphasize part of a word, like the first syllable of the English word accent.

There are also the letter **ç c cedilha** (*c cedilla*), which makes the **c** soft, and the dieresis (two dots, like the German umlaut) to denote words of non-Portuguese origin in their original forms (e.g. **Müller**).

STRESS

Portuguese words are classified into three groups in terms of where the stress (emphasis) falls:

1 **last syllable**

2 **penultimate (next to last)**

3 **antepenultimate (third-last)**

The majority belong to Group 2 and do not usually require a written accent. The written accent occurs to enable words to be correctly stressed when they have deviated from the usual stress pattern. Whenever you see a written accent, that is where you should emphasize the word when you say it. Words also carry a written stress mark to distinguish them from a word with the same spelling but a different meaning, e.g. **por** (*by*) and **pôr** (*to put*). These are relatively rare.

A FEW TIPS TO HELP YOU ACQUIRE AN AUTHENTIC ACCENT

It is not absolutely vital to acquire a perfect accent – the aim is to be understood. Here are a number of techniques for working on your pronunciation:

1 Listen carefully to the audio, Brazilian Portuguese speaker or teacher. Whenever possible repeat out loud, imagining you are a Brazilian Portuguese speaker.

2 Record yourself and compare your pronunciation with that of a Brazilian Portuguese speaker.

3 Ask Brazilian Portuguese speakers to listen to your pronunciation and tell you how to improve it.

4 Ask Brazilian Portuguese speakers how a specific sound is formed. Watch them and practice at home in front of a mirror.

5 Make a list of words that give you pronunciation trouble and practice them.

Useful expressions

00.02 NUMBERS

1	**um / uma**
2	**dois**
3	**três**
4	**quatro**
5	**cinco**
6	**seis**
7	**sete**
8	**oito**
9	**nove**
10	**dez**
11	**onze**
12	**doze**
13	**treze**
14	**quatorze / catorze**
15	**quinze**
16	**dezesseis**
17	**dezessete**
18	**dezoito**
19	**dezenove**
20	**vinte**
21	**vinte e um / uma**
22	**vinte e dois / duas**
23	**vinte e três**
24	**vinte e quatro**
25	**vinte e cinco**

This pattern is maintained throughout all the tens, through to 99.

30	**trinta**	178	**cento e setenta e oito**
40	**quarenta**	182	**cento e oitenta e dois / duas**
50	**cinquenta**	199	**cento e noventa e nove**
60	**sessenta**	200	**duzentos / duzentas**
70	**setenta**	300	**trezentos / trezentas**
80	**oitenta**	400	**quatrocentos / quatrocentas**
90	**noventa**	500	**quinhentos / quinhentas**
100	**cem**	600	**seiscentos / seiscentas**
101	**cento e um / uma**	700	**setecentos / setecentas**
102	**cento e dois / duas**	800	**oitocentos / oitocentas**
125	**cento e vinte e cinco**	900	**novecentos / novecentas**
146	**cento e quarenta e seis**	1,000	**mil**
163	**cento e sessenta e três**		

00.03 DAYS OF THE WEEK

Sunday	**domingo**
Monday	**segunda-feira**
Tuesday	**terça-feira**
Wednesday	**quarta-feira**
Thursday	**quinta-feira**
Friday	**sexta-feira**
Saturday	**sábado**

MONTHS OF THE YEAR

January	**janeiro**
February	**fevereiro**
March	**março**
April	**abril**
May	**maio**
June	**junho**
July	**julho**
August	**agosto**

September	**setembro**
October	**outubro**
November	**novembro**
December	**dezembro**

00.04 EVERYDAY EXPRESSIONS

Can you repeat that, please?	**Pode repetir, por favor?**
Once more, please.	**Mais uma vez, por favor.**
Speak more slowly, please.	**Fale mais devagar, por favor.**
Do you understand?	**Você entende?**
I understand.	**Entendo.**
I don't understand.	**Não entendo.**
I don't know.	**Não sei.**
Is that correct?	**Está certo?**
That's right.	**Está certo. / Isso!**
Do you speak English?	**Você fala inglês?**
Do you speak Portuguese?	**Você fala português?**
I speak Portuguese, but not very well.	**Falo português, mas não muito bem.**
How much does it cost?	**Quanto custa?**
Where is ...?	**Onde fica ...? / Onde é ...?**
I'm sorry!	**Desculpe!**
What time is it?	**Que horas são?**

GENERAL GREETINGS

Hi!	**Oi!**
Good morning. / Hello.	**Bom dia.**
Good afternoon. / Hello. (usually up to early evening)	**Boa tarde.**
Good evening. / Good night.	**Boa noite.**
Everything OK?	**Tudo bem?**
How are you?	**Como você está?**
I'm well. / I'm fine.	**Estou bem.**

Thank you. (said by a woman)	**Obrigada.**
Thank you. (said by a man)	**Obrigado.**
yes	**sim**
no	**não**
See you later.	**Até logo.**
See you tomorrow.	**Até amanhã.**
Goodbye.	**Adeus. / Tchau!**
Let's go!	**Vamos!**

BASIC QUESTIONS

How?	**Como?**
Who?	**Quem?**
When?	**Quando?**
Where?	**Onde?**
What ... / Which ...?	**Que ... / O que ...?**
Which (one / ones)?	**Qual? / Quais?**
Why ...?	**Por que ...?**
How much / How many?	**Quanto / Quanta / Quantos / Quantas?**

In this unit you will learn how to:

» say *hello* and *goodbye*.
» introduce yourself and others.
» say where you come from and what languages you speak.
» say what your job or profession is.
» use the present tense of verbs.
» ask questions.

Como vai?

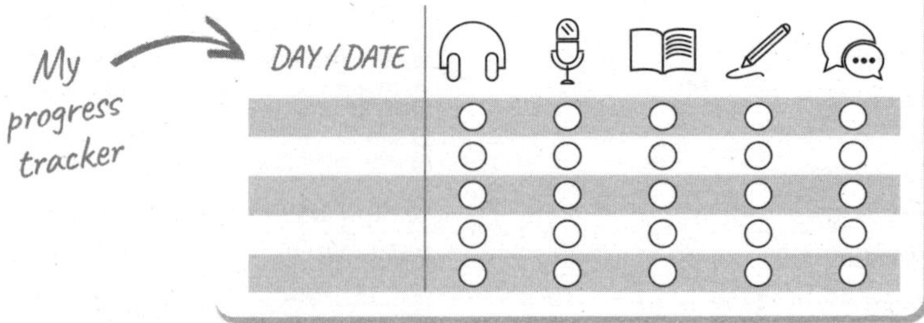

Brazil

O Brasil (*Brazil*) is the largest country in **América do Sul** (*South America*). It has borders with all the other South American countries, except with Chile and Ecuador. Brazil's rate of population growth has decreased dramatically in the last few decades due to the process of urbanization and modernization.

Brazil is divided into 26 **estados** (*states*) and one **Distrito Federal** (*Federal District*) where the capital, Brasília, is located. Most Brazilians live in the **região Sudeste** (*South East region*) and in the **Nordeste** (*North East region*).

About 0.8 per cent of the total population are **índios** (*Indians*) – most live in indigenous protected areas. Brazil has the largest number of people of Japanese ancestry outside Japan – most of them live in the state of São Paulo, along with large communities of descendants of **sírios** (*Syrians*), **libaneses** (*Lebanese*), **italianos** (*Italians*), **alemães** (*Germans*) and other European immigrants who entered Brazil in the 18th, 19th and 20th centuries.

Can you guess what the names of the other three regions of Brazil mean: região Sul, região Norte and região Centro-Oeste?

Vocabulary builder

01.01 Look at the words and phrases and complete the missing English expressions. Then listen and try to imitate the pronunciation of the speakers.

CUMPRIMENTOS	*GREETINGS*
Bom dia	*Good morning.*
Boa tarde	*Good afternoon. / Good evening.*
Boa noite	_______ *evening* (later) */night.*
Oi	*Hi / Hello.*
Tudo bem? / Tudo bem	*Everything's OK? / Everything's fine.*
Como está?	*How are you?* (more formal)
Como vai?	_______ *are you?* (less formal)
Muito prazer	*Pleased to meet you.*
Até logo	*See you later / soon.*
Até amanhã	*See you tomorrow.*
Até mais tarde	_______ *later.*
Tchau!	*Bye!*
Adeus	*Goodbye.*

PERGUNTAS	*QUESTIONS*
Qual é o seu nome?	*What's your name?*
Como se chama?	*What are you called?*
Onde trabalha?	*Where do you work?*
O que faz?	*What (work) do you do?*
Qual é o seu email?	*What's your email?*
Você fala (espanhol)?	*Do you speak (Spanish)?*

NEW EXPRESSIONS

01.02 Look at the words and expressions that are used in the following conversation. Note their meanings.

Como está a senhora?	*How are you (madam)?*
Estou bem	*I'm well.*
E o senhor, como vai?	*And you (sir), how are you?*
Obrigado/ obrigada	*Thank you.* (m/f)

Desculpe	*Excuse me / I'm sorry.*
Qual é o nome da senhora?	*What's your name (madam)?* (formal)
Chamo-me ...	*I'm called ...*
Trabalho por conta própria	*I work for myself.*
(Eu) sou ...	*I am (I'm) ...*
Trabalho para ...	*I work for ...*
Que interessante!	*How interesting!*
Este é o meu colega	*This is my colleague.*
Ele também é ...	*He is also a ... / He's a ... too.*
Ótimo!	*Great! / Brilliant!*
Então	*Well then / So / In that case.*

Conversation 1

01.03 *At a business meeting in Curitiba,* **senhor** *(Mr) Silva and* **senhora** *(Mrs) Costa chat during a coffee break.*

1 What is senhora Costa's first name?

Sr Silva	Bom dia. Como está a senhora?
Sra Costa	Bom dia. Estou bem, obrigada, e o senhor, como vai?
Sr Silva	Vou bem, obrigado. Desculpe, qual é o nome da senhora?
Sra Costa	Chamo-me Ana Costa. E o senhor?
Sr Silva	Paulo Silva. Onde a senhora trabalha?
Sra Costa	Trabalho por conta própria – sou advogada. E o senhor? O que faz?
Sr Silva	Eu sou engenheiro. Trabalho para Renault.
Sra Costa	Que interessante!
(Senhor Silva spots a colleague and introduces senhora Costa to him).	
Sr Silva	Senhora Costa, este é o meu colega, José dos Santos. Ele também é engenheiro.
Sra Costa	Muito prazer!
Sr Silva	Ótimo! Então, até mais tarde.
Sra Costa	Até logo!

2 Read the conversation again, and with the help of the new expressions, answer the questions.

a What time of day does the conversation take place?

b What is senhora Costa's profession?

c What is the name of senhor Silva's colleague?

3 Answer true or false to the following statements.

- **a** Senhora Costa works for herself.
- **b** Senhor Silva is a lawyer.
- **c** Senhora Costa says *See you tomorrow*.

4 Now listen to the conversation again, repeating after each line, and concentrating on your pronunciation.

LANGUAGE TIP

To call someone *you* in Brazil, use **o senhor** for men, and **a senhora** for women, in situations requiring formality and polite exchange, such as with strangers and in business meetings; **senhor** and **senhora** also mean *Mr* and *Mrs*. You will hear most Brazilians call each other **você** for *you*, which is less formal.
Many Brazilians say **Eu me chamo X**, instead of **Chamo-me X**.

Language discovery 1

1 Identify the words for *I* and *he* in these expressions from the conversation:

- **a** Eu sou engenheiro (*I am an engineer*).
- **b** Ele é engenheiro (*He is an engineer*).

2 Which Portuguese words translate the verb *I am* in the following expressions?

- **a** estou bem
- **b** sou engenheiro

3 Look at these expressions from the conversation, and decide why the words in bold change in form:

- **a** Como **está** a senhora? (*How are you?*)
- **b** **Estou** bem, obrigada. (*I'm well, thank you*)

1 PERSONAL (SUBJECT) PRONOUNS

In Portuguese, the words for *I*, *you*, *he*, etc., also called subject pronouns, are not always needed, as the ending of the verbs (action words) indicates who is carrying out the action. They are needed, however, to avoid ambiguity, when some verb forms are identical, and they can also be used for emphasis. Here are the subject pronouns you will use in Brazilian Portuguese:

eu	*I*	**nós**	*we*
você[1]	*you* (sing)	**vocês**[1]	*you* (pl)
ele / ela	*he / she / it*[2]	**eles**[3] **/ elas**	*they*

[1] use **o senhor / a senhora** and the plurals **os senhores / as senhoras** in formal situations, but follow the same verb endings as for **você / vocês**.

[2] both **ele** and **ela** are used to mean *it*, depending on the gender of the word in question.

[3] **eles** is used for groups of two or more males and mixed groups of males and females.

2 THE VERB *TO BE* – SER

Portuguese has two verbs meaning *to be*: **ser** and **estar**. **Ser** is used for permanent characteristics; use it to give your profession, or nationality.

eu sou	*I am*	**nós somos**	*we are*
você é	*you are* (sing)	**vocês são**	*you are* (pl)
ele / ela é	*he / she / it is*	**eles / elas são**	*they are*

PROFISSÕES E COMÉRCIOS

masculine	feminine	
médico	**médica**	*doctor*
professor	**professora**	*teacher*
enfermeiro	**enfermeira**	*nurse*
gerente de operações	**gerente de operações**	*operations manager*
técnico de informática	**técnica de informática**	*IT technician*
eletricista	**eletricista**	*electrician*
cozinheiro	**cozinheira**	*cook*

You don't need to say the word for *a* before your profession in Portuguese; simply state, for example, *I am teacher*.

3 THE VERB *TO BE* – ESTAR

Estar is used for situations of a more temporary nature; use it to ask how someone is or to enquire where someone is.

eu estou	**nós estamos**
você está	**vocês estão**
ele / ela está	**eles / elas estão**

Here are some interesting uses of the verb **estar**:

estar com fome — *to be hungry*

estar com frio — *to be cold* (person)

estar com calor — *to be hot* (person)

estar com pressa — *to be in a hurry*

estar com sede — *to be thirsty*

These literally mean *to be with hunger, with cold*, etc.

Practice 1

1 Complete each sentence using one of the words from the box.

eu	você	nós	ele

a _______ está bem?
b Este é José; _______ é engenheiro de software.
c _______ sou administrador de banco de dados (database administrator).
d _______ estamos bem.

2 Complete the missing words.

	masculine	feminine	English
a	**médico**	_______	*doctor*
b	**professor**	**professora**	_______
c	_______	**gerente**	*manager*
d	**enfermeiro**	_______	*nurse*
e	_______	**dentista**	*dentist*

3 Choose the correct verb (ser or estar) for each sentence.

a Como é / está o senhor?
b Sou / Estou designer gráfico.
c Estou / Sou bem, obrigada.
d Ela também é / está assistente social (*social worker*).

4 Match the Portuguese and English.

a	Nós estamos com fome.	**1**	Are you in a hurry?
b	Ela está com calor?	**2**	I am thirsty.
c	Você está com pressa?	**3**	We are hungry.
d	Eu estou com sede.	**4**	Is she hot?

5 01.04 Listen for people's nationalities and their professions.

		Nacionalidade	O que faz?
a	**Ana**	_______	_______
b	**Peter**	_______	_______
c	**Isabel**	_______	_______
d	**Paulo**	_______	_______

6 01.05 Listen and fill in the gaps with the missing words.

a Meu _______ é João Mendes da Silva.
b Sou _______ São Paulo, mas _______ em Brasília.
c _______ dentista e trabalho por conta _______.
d Sou recepcionista; _______ Mônica.
e Ela _______ portuguesa.

7 **01.06 What is the matter with each person? Circle the correct answer.**

a Carlos is	thirsty	in a hurry	cold
b Joaquim is	hot	hungry	thirsty
c Anita is	cold	hungry	in a hurry
d Catarina is	hot	thirsty	in a hurry

Conversation 2

01.07 *Some international research students exchange information about themselves at their first seminar.*

Read and listen to the conversation, then answer the questions.

1 What languages does Bruno speak?

Ornella	Oi, tudo bem?
Bruno	Tudo bem. Qual é o seu nome?
Ornella	Eu sou Ornella. E você?
Bruno	Meu nome é Bruno. De onde você é, Ornella?
Ornella	Eu sou italiana, de Roma. E você?
Bruno	Sou francês, de Toulouse.
Ornella	Você fala inglês?
Bruno	Falo, sim – inglês e também espanhol. E você?
Ornella	Bem, falo inglês e alemão.
Bruno	Ornella, você está em alguma rede social?
Ornella	Não, não estou.
Bruno	Então, qual é o número do seu celular?
Ornella	É 0797-33314558

(Bruno spots his friend, Mônica, approaching, and introduces Ornella to her).

Bruno	Ah, Ornella, esta é a minha amiga, Mônica – ela é argentina.
Ornella	Tudo bem Mônica?

2 Read the conversation again and choose the correct answer to the questions.

a What nationality is Ornella?	Spanish / Italian
b Which city is Bruno from?	Rome / Toulouse
c Which languages does Ornella speak?	English and French / English and German

- **d** Is Ornella on any social media network? Yes / No
- **e** Whose phone number is 0797-33314558? Bruno's / Ornella's
- **f** Where is Mônica from? USA / Argentina

Language discovery 2

1 Find the expressions in the conversation which mean:

- **a** Do you speak English?
- **b** I speak English.

2 In the conversation, Bruno says Sou francês ... falo ... inglês (*I am French ... I speak ... English*). What do you think it would mean if someone were to say Sou inglês ... falo francês?

> You may not always hear the little words **o** and **a** in the expressions **o meu**, **o seu**, **a minha**, and so on; some Brazilians don't include them at all.

1 PRESENT TENSE OF VERBS ENDING IN -AR

The present tense of verbs is used to describe actions you carry out regularly or which are a statement of fact. Look at how it works with a verb ending in -ar.

Remove the **-ar** then add the following endings:

falar *to speak*			
eu	**fal + o = falo** *I speak*	**nós**	**fal + amos = falamos** *we speak*
você	**fal + a = fala** *you speak* (sing)	**vocês**	**fal + am = falam** *you speak* (pl)
ele / ela	**fal + a = fala** *he / she / it speaks*	**eles / elas**	**fal+am = falam** *they speak*

To make a verb negative, put the word **não** before it

não falo inglês *I don't speak English*

To make a question with the verb, simply lift up the intonation of your voice at the end of the sentence to make it sound like a question. Portuguese does not translate the equivalent of the English *do ...?* or *does ...?*

não	*no / not*
sim	*yes*

2 LANGUAGES AND NATIONALITIES

The language of a country is the same word in Portuguese as the masculine form of the nationality. When talking about the nationality of women, you need to use the feminine version of the word. Look at these examples and keep an eye out for similar patterns:

language	masculine nationality	feminine nationality	
italiano	**italiano**	**italiana**	*Italian*
inglês	**inglês**	**inglesa**	*English*
espanhol	**espanhol**	**espanhola**	*Spanish*
alemão	**alemão**	**alemã**	*German*

Falo um pouco de italiano. *I speak a bit of Italian.*

Falo francês bem. *I speak French well.*

Não falo inglês muito bem. *I don't speak English very well.*

Practice 2

1 Add the correct verb endings.

- **a** Eu fal _______ inglês.
- **b** Elas não fal _______ japonês (*Japanese*).
- **c** O senhor fal _______ russo (*Russian*).
- **d** Nós não fal _______ norueguês (*Norwegian*).

2 Make the sentences negative.

- **a** Você é de Londres (*London*).
- **b** Meu nome é Kofi.
- **c** Paulo fala alemão.
- **d** Ela é coreana (*Korean*).

3 Complete the words of nationality.

- **a** __t__li__na
- **b** al__ __ã__
- **c** f__ __nc__s
- **d** es__an__ol__

4 Translate the following sentences and then say them out loud in Portuguese.

- **a** I speak a bit of Portuguese.
- **b** I don't speak Japanese.
- **c** We speak French well.

Reading

Pedro introduces himself:

Olá! Sou Pedro Rodrigues de Carvalho. Sou brasileiro, de Campinas, mas (*but*) agora moro (*I live*) em São José dos Campos. Sou engenheiro mecânico e trabalho na Embraer. Falo um pouco de espanhol e um pouco de inglês. Este é o meu amigo Eduardo Watanabe. Ele também trabalha na Embraer. Ele é fluente em inglês.

According to the text, are these statements true or false?

- **a** Pedro was born in São José dos Campos.
- **b** Pedro speaks English fluently.
- **c** Pedro is an engineer.
- **d** His friend does not work at Embraer.

Reading and writing

Sou de Uberlândia, mas agora moro em Belo Horizonte.

I am from Uberlândia, but now I live in Belo Horizonte.

Using this sentence as a model, fill in the gaps in the following sentences with the words that are missing. Then try to create sentences by following the instructions.

- **a** Sou de Recife, mas ________ moro ________ Salvador.
- **b** Sou ________ Belém, ________ agora moro em Chicago.
- **c** ________ de Ubatuba, mas agora ________ em São Paulo.
- **d** Translate: *I am from Brasília, but now I live in London.*

  ____

- **e** Create a sentence yourself, following the same pattern.

  ____

Speaking

1 Try to answer these questions in Portuguese.

- **a** Você é australiana?
- **b** Você fala inglês?
- **c** O Roberto é de São Paulo?
- **d** Onde você mora?
- **e** A Cristina tem perfil no Instagram (*a profile on Instagram*)?

2 01.08 Pronunciation practice

The following words from the conversations all had the letter combination **nh** in them: **senhor**, **senhora**, **engenheiro**, **espanhol**, **cozinheira**. It sounds like the *ni* sound in the English word *onion*. Listen to them again now and repeat them, concentrating hard on sounding like the speaker.

Go further

In Brazil, people tend to have two or more **sobrenomes** (*surnames*), at least one from the mother and one from the father – for example **Sônia Macedo da Silva**. Many Brazilians have non-Brazilian surnames – German, Italian, Polish, Japanese – reflecting the origin of their grandparents or great-grandparents. Some have unusual first names, made up by the parents, including non-Brazilian names written as they sound to them in Portuguese, such as **Uoshinton**, **Maicon**, **Madenusa**, **Djenifer** and other creations. When discussing people using first names, it is common to insert **o** before male names, and **a** before female names, such as **o Pedro** and **a Ana**, although not all Brazilians do this.

Test yourself

1 Match each question on the left to the corresponding correct answer on the right.

- **a** Como se chama?
- **b** Onde trabalha?
- **c** O que faz?
- **d** Qual é o seu email?
- **e** Você fala alemão?

- **1** Trabalho por conta própria.
- **2** É pedro.paulo@outlook.com
- **3** Sim, falo um pouco.
- **4** Chamo-me Alberto.
- **5** Sou arquiteto.

2 Fill the gaps to complete the sentences.

- **a** Bom ________. ________ vai?
- **b** ________ é meu colega.
- **c** Oi, ________ bem?
- **d** ________ prazer!
- **e** Eu ________ fluente em inglês.
- **f** O gerente ________ japonês.

3 **Make the sentences plural.**

a O novo engenheiro é coreano.
b Ela não fala português.
c Ele está com fome.

SELF CHECK

I CAN ...
... say *hello* and *goodbye*.
... introduce myself and others.
... say where I come from and what languages I speak.
... say what my job or profession is.
... use the present tense of verbs.
... ask questions.

2

In this unit, you will learn how to:

» talk about how old people are.
» talk about your family.
» express marital status.
» use numbers from 0 to 100.
» describe people.
» discuss where people are studying.

Família e amigos

My progress tracker

DAY / DATE

Os brasileiros

Brazilians are very sociable and family-oriented. They like to speak about themselves and their **famílias** (*families*) and are very interested in getting to know people from other parts of the **país** (*country*) and of the **mundo** (*world*). They will be curious to know if you are **solteiro** (*single*) or **casado** (*married*), if you have children, where you live, what you do for a living and other information that you may consider intrusive, but they just want to get to know you and perhaps make a new **amigo** (*friend*). Very few Brazilians can speak English fluently – most can speak only a few words or sentences – so you will need to speak Portuguese if you want to make the most of your stay in Brazil.

Many Brazilians are **funcionários públicos** (*civil servants*) as those jobs tend to be more stable and secure. Selection for these jobs is made at national, state and municipal levels through an exam known as the **concurso público**, designed according to each position – some will require a university degree, others secondary school or primary school level. Post office workers, teachers in state schools and universities, police officers and judges all have to pass a similar exam.

At the end of **ensino médio** (*secondary school*), students sit a national exam called **ENEM**. You can enter some Universities if you have a very good score on the ENEM exam. Some Universities have their own entrance exam, called **VESTIBULAR**.

Can you guess what João is saying about himself? Sou solteiro, sou funcionário público e não falo inglês.

Vocabulary builder

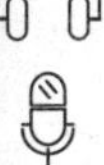

02.01 **Look at the words and phrases and complete the missing English expressions. Then listen and try to imitate the pronunciation of the speakers.**

A FAMÍLIA	*THE FAMILY*
o marido / o esposo	*husband*
a mulher / a esposa	*wife*
o namorado	*boyfriend*
a namorada	________
o pai / a mãe	*father / mother*
o filho / a filha	*son /* ________
o irmão / a irmã	*brother /* ________
o padrasto	*stepfather*
a madrasta	*stepmother*
o sogro / a sogra	*father / mother in law*
o genro / a nora	*son / daughter in law*
o enteado / a enteada	*stepson / stepdaughter*

NEW EXPRESSIONS

02.02 **Look at the words and expressions that are used in the following conversation. Note their meanings.**

Você é casado?	*Are you married?*
Qual é o nome dela?	*What's her name?*
Tenho uma foto dela	*I have a photo of her.*
Você tem filhos?	*Do you have (any) children?*
um filho só	*one son only / just one son*
Quantos anos ele tem?	*How old is he?* (lit. *How many years does he have?*)
... está no segundo ano de Direito	*... is in the second year of Law*
... quer ser advogado	*... wants to be a lawyer*

... é mais velho	*... is older*
tem o seu próprio negócio	*he has his own business*
ele vende peças de automóveis	*he sells motor car parts*
Ah é?	*Really? / Is that so?*
aqui vem	*here comes*
Oi querida! Então?	*Hi darling! Well then?*

Conversation 1

02.03 *Rosa and Fernando are waiting for their partners after a meeting; they chat about their families.*

1 What is Fernando's girlfriend called?

Rosa	Então, Fernando, você é casado?
Fernando	Casado, não; sou separado, mas tenho uma namorada.
Rosa	Qual é o nome dela?
Fernando	Ela se chama Luciana. Tenho uma foto dela aqui no celular.
Rosa	Você tem filhos, Fernando?
Fernando	Tenho, sim – um filho só.
Rosa	Quantos anos ele tem?
Fernando	O Felipe tem dezenove anos, está no segundo ano de Direito; quer ser advogado.
Rosa	Eu tenho uma filha que também é estudante. O meu filho, Marcelo, é mais velho; tem o seu próprio negócio; ele vende peças de automóveis.
Fernando	Ah é?
(Rosa sees her husband approaching).	
Rosa	Ah, aqui vem o meu marido. Paulo, estamos aqui!
Paulo	Oi querida! E então?
Rosa	Paulo, este é o Fernando. Ele trabalha para o Banco do Brasil.
Paulo	Muito prazer.

2 Read the conversation again and, with the help of the new expressions, answer the questions.

a Does Fernando have any children?

b Who is 19 years old?

c Who is Paulo?

3 Now listen to the conversation again, repeating after each line and concentrating on your pronunciation.

LANGUAGE TIP

The plural of **filho** (*son*), **filhos**, can mean *sons* or *sons and daughters*. **Pais** means *parents*, and **irmãos** means either *brothers* or *brothers and sisters*.
To express marital status, use: **casado** (*married*), **divorciado** (*divorced*), **solteiro** (*single*), **separado** (*separated*) or **viúvo** (*widowed*). Change the final **-o** of each word to an **-a** to describe a woman's status.

Language discovery 1

1 **Identify the Portuguese verb for** *I have* **in the following expression:**
tenho uma namorada tenho uma foto

2 **Which Portuguese word means** *he sells* **in the following expression?**
... vende peças de automóveis.

3 **Which two words in the conversation mean** *a*, **as in** *a son and a daughter*, **and why do you think there are two versions of the word in Portuguese?**

1 THE VERB *TO HAVE* – TER

The Portuguese verb *to have*, **ter**, is formed as follows:

eu tenho	*I have*	**nós temos**	*we have*
você tem	*you have* (sing)	**vocês têm**	*you have* (pl)
ele / ela tem	*he / she / it has*	**eles / elas têm**	*they have*

This is the everyday verb to express what you have or do not have. For example, *I have a son*; *I have a photo*.

LANGUAGE TIP

The verb **ter** is also used in the expression for talking about age. **Quantos anos você tem?** *How old are you?* (lit. *How many years do you have?*) **Tenho 50 anos.** *I am 50* (lit. *I have 50 years*).

2 A REGULAR -ER ENDING VERB – PRESENT TENSE

Many regular verbs in Portuguese fall into the group ending in **-er**, which are formed as follows: first, remove the **-er**, then add endings to what is left (known as the stem) to denote who is carrying out the action.

Look at the verb *to sell*, **vender**:

vender – er = vend (stem)			
eu vendo	*I sell*	**nós vendemos**	*we sell*
você vende	*you sell* (sing)	**vocês vendem**	*you sell* (pl)
ele / ela vende	*he / she / it sells*	**eles / elas vendem**	*they sell* (pl)

3 HOW TO TRANSLATE *A / AN* AND *THE*

The Portuguese words for *a / an* and *the* have to match the item they are with in terms of whether they are masculine or feminine, and singular or plural:

	masculine	feminine	masculine plural	feminine plural
a / an, some	**um**	**uma**	**uns***	**umas***
the	**o**	**a**	**os**	**as**

*the plurals **uns** and **umas** are sometimes replaced by the alternative words for *some*, **alguns** and **algumas**. In other situations, they are often just omitted.

A brother is **um irmão**, *the daughters* **as filhas**. As you go along, make sure you learn whether each noun (word for a thing, person or concept) is masculine or feminine by checking in the word lists or a dictionary.

NUMBERS 0–100

You may need to refresh your memory on number formation by looking back to the introductory material of this course and listening to the numbers on the audio. Here are some sample numbers to help you. Look at the patterns of formation to help you remember them:

0 **zero**
1 **um**
2 **dois***
3 **três**
4 **quatro**
5 **cinco**
6 **seis**
7 **sete**
8 **oito**
9 **nove**
10 **dez**

11 **onze**
12 **doze**
13 **treze**
14 **quatorze / catorze**
15 **quinze**
16 **dezesseis**
17 **dezessete**
18 **dezoito**
19 **dezenove**
20 **vinte**

21 **vinte e um**
34 **trinta e quatro**
46 **quarenta e seis**
58 **cinquenta e oito**
60 **sessenta**
72 **setenta e dois**
83 **oitenta e três**
95 **noventa e cinco**
100 **cem**

*the number two has a masculine form (**dois**) and a feminine (**duas**). Use the masculine form for normal counting, money and years; use the feminine version when referring to anything feminine, e.g., **duas filhas** *two daughters.*

primeiro *first*
segundo *second*
terceiro *third*

Practice 1

1 Complete each sentence by choosing the correct part of the verb ter.

- **a** Quantos anos você tem / têm ?
- **b** Eu tenho / tem 19 anos.
- **c** Nós têm / temos seis primos (*cousins*).
- **d** O José tem / tenho o seu próprio negócio.
- **e** Vocês tem / têm um apartamento na praia?
- **f** Ela não tem / tenho Instagram.

2 Correctly form the verbs to complete the sentences.

- **a** (vender *to sell*) Ela _______ produtos de limpeza (*cleaning products*).
- **b** (comer *to eat*) Eu _______ bananas.
- **c** (beber *to drink*) Vocês _______ café (*coffee*)?
- **d** (escrever *to write*) Nós _______ uma mensagem (*a message*).
- **e** (correr *to run*) O Isaque _______ na praia (*on the beach*).

3 Make the statements singular. Follow the example.

as irmãs → a irmã

- **a** meus irmãos → _______
- **b** as fotos → _______
- **c** os funcionários públicos → _______
- **d** as mães → _______

4 What is the number?

- **a** cento e vinte e cinco _______
- **b** cinquenta e quatro _______
- **c** setenta e sete _______
- **d** quinhentos e dez _______

5 02.04 Now listen to Fábio speaking about himself and his family. Then answer the questions.

nós dois	*both of us*
Universidade Federal	*Federal University*

- **a** How old is Fábio?
- **b** What is he studying at university?
- **c** How old is his sister Heloísa?
- **d** What does their mother do?

Conversation 2

02.05 *Two friends, Mateus and Simone, are looking at family photos on their mobile phones.*

Read and listen to the conversation, then answer the questions.

1 How old is Marcela?

Mateus	Olha, gente! Tenho aqui umas fotos da minha namorada e dos meus irmãos.
Simone	A sua namorada é alta e bonita. O que ela faz?
Mateus	Ela é engenheira de software. Este é o meu irmão Cauã, mais velho que eu.
Simone	Nossa, que gato! Ele está aqui no Rio?
Mateus	Não. Ele está no Canadá. Ele é influenciador digital e tem um canal no YouTube. Esta aqui é a minha irmã Marcela. Ela tem vinte e dois anos. É mais nova que eu.
Simone	Ela está no Brasil ou também está no Canadá?
Mateus	No Canadá, num intercâmbio de seis meses. Nesta foto ela tem cabelos castanhos, mas agora tem cabelos ruivos!
Simone	Eu também tenho uma foto aqui. Esta é a minha mãe, este é meu padrasto e estes são os meus primos e tios de Belo Horizonte.
Mateus	Onde estão nesta foto?
Simone	Em Ouro Preto. Que cidade linda!

2 Read the conversation again and answer the statements with True or False.

a Mateus' girlfriend is a software engineer. ________

b Cauã is not in Brazil. ________

c Marcela is Mateus' girlfriend. ________

d Marcela has a YouTube channel. ________

e Simone has been to Ouro Preto. ________

AUTHENTIC EXPRESSIONS

Nossa!	*Wow!*
Gente!	*Folks! / Gang! / You guys!*
Olha gente! / Olhe gente!	*Look, everyone / guys! / Look here!*
Que gato / gata!	*He's / She's really gorgeous!* (lit. *What a cat!*)
Que lindo!	*He's so handsome! / It's so pretty!*

DESCRIBING EYES

tem os olhos ... azuis / verdes / pretos / castanhos	*he / she has blue / green / dark (black) / brown eyes*

DESCRIBING HAIR COLOUR

tem os cabelos *(hair)* **pretos / castanhos / loiros / ruivos** OR **tem o cabelo preto / castanho / loiro / ruivo**	*he / she has black / brown / blonde / red hair*

DESCRIBING PEOPLE

alto	*tall*
baixo	*short*
moreno	*tanned*

Change the final **-o** to **-a** to describe a woman.

Language discovery 2

1 **Which word for** *pretty* **is used to describe Mateus' girlfriend?**

2 **In the conversation, find the Portuguese expression for** *older*.

3 **Can you find in the dialogue the equivalent in Portuguese for** *six months*?

4 **Why do you think there is a difference between the expressions for** *my* **in the following:**

o meu irmão (*my brother*) **os meus primos** (*my cousins*)

1 ADJECTIVES (DESCRIBING WORDS)

Words which describe (adjectives), such as *tall, short, old, young*, etc., change their ending in Portuguese to match what they are describing in terms of whether the thing or person is masculine, feminine, singular or plural. Most regular Portuguese adjectives end in **-o**, and form their changes like this:

	masc. sing.	fem. sing.	masc. pl.	fem.pl
alto (*tall*)	**alto**	**alta**	**altos**	**altas**

2 COMPARATIVES: EXPRESSING *OLDER, YOUNGER, WISER*, ETC.

To say something is *older*, *younger*, *cheaper*, etc., in Portuguese you use the word for *more* (**mais**), with the appropriate adjective, remembering to change its ending if necessary.

ela é mais alta *she is taller*

vocês são mais velhos *you are older*

Note the following word order: **a Akira é a minha irmã mais velha** *Akira is my older sister* (lit. *Akira is my sister more old*). The word used for *young*, **novo**, actually means *new*.

3 THE VERB *TO DO / TO MAKE* – FAZER

The Portuguese verb **fazer** means *to do* or *to make*. It is widely used, so now's a good time to learn it.

eu faço	*I do / make*	**nós fazemos**	*we do / make*
você faz	*you do / make* (sing)	**vocês fazem**	*you do / make* (pl)
ele / ela faz	*he / she / it does / makes*	**eles / elas fazem**	*they do / make*

Use **fazer** to say when your birthday is: **faço aniversário em setembro** *it's my birthday in September*. Go back to the introductory material of this course to remind yourself how to say the months of the year in Portuguese.

4 WORDS OF POSSESSION (*MY, YOUR, OUR*) – AN INTRODUCTORY SUMMARY

The words of possession in Portuguese match the words that are being possessed, not the person, or thing, doing the possessing. Look at the patterns to help you remember them.

	masc. sing.	fem. sing.	masc. pl.	fem. pl.
my	**o meu**	**a minha**	**os meus**	**as minhas**
your	**o seu**	**a sua**	**os seus**	**as suas**
our	**o nosso**	**a nossa**	**os nossos**	**as nossas**

Often, Brazilians leave out the words **o**, **a**, etc.

my father **(o) meu pai**

your girlfriend **(a) sua namorada**

our sons / children **(os) nossos filhos**

Practice 2

1 Find the correct adjective for each expression.

a	É uma casa (*house*)	**1**	baixo
b	Os irmãos são	**2**	bonita
c	O meu pai é	**3**	baratas (*cheap*)
d	As botas (*boots*) são	**4**	idosos (*elderly*)

2 Match the Portuguese sentence with its English translation.

a	Ela é mais baixa.	**1**	The fattest cats.
b	Este é o meu irmão mais novo.	**2**	This is my younger brother.
c	Os gatos mais gordos.	**3**	She is shorter.
d	As praias mais lindas.	**4**	The prettiest beaches.

3 Translate using the verb fazer. Say your answers out loud.

a My birthday's in March.
b His birthday's in December.
c When is your birthday?
d They make a good coffee.

4 Change from singular to plural.

a a minha irmã → _______
b o seu empregado → _______
c a nossa casa → _______
d o meu tio *(uncle)* → _______

Reading and writing

1 Fill in the gaps in the text, choosing the correct word from the box.

em tenho dois sou no é minha de

Meu nome _______ Ângela dos Santos Macedo. Moro _______ São Paulo, mas sou _______ Taubaté. _______ vinte e cinco anos e _______ solteira. Moro com meu pai, _______ mãe e meus _______ irmãos: Paulo e Flávio. Sou recepcionista no Hotel Transamérica. Tenho um perfil _____ Instagram e um canal no YouTube.

(*perfil* - *profile*)

2 According to the text, what are the correct answers to the following questions?

a How old is Ângela?

b Where was she born?

c Is she married or single?

d Where does she live?

3 02.06 **Pronunciation practice**

The following words from the conversations all had the letter combination **lh** in them: **filho**, **filha**, **velho**, **olhos**, **trabalha**. This sounds like the *lli* sound in the English word *million*. Listen to these words again now and repeat them, concentrating hard on sounding like the speaker.

Go further

Here are some further phrases to describe yourself and other people:

eu tenho ...	*I have ...*
ele / ela tem ...	*he / she has ...*
cabelos brancos / grisalhos	*white / grey hair*
cabelos longos	*long hair*
cabelos curtos	*short hair*
barba	*beard*
bigode	*moustache*
eu sou ...	*I am ...*
ele / ela é ...	*he / she is ...*
careca	*bald*
eu uso ...	*I wear / use*
ele / ela usa ...	*he / she wears / uses*
óculos	*glasses*
lentes de contato	*contact lenses*
chapéu	*hat*
bengala	*walking stick / cane*

Could you describe yourself, using the vocabulary given?

Eu tenho cabelos ________, olhos ________. Sou ________.

Uso / Não uso ________.

Listen and understand

02.07 **Listen to three people describing their relatives and identify them amongst the pictures.**

Test yourself

1 Follow the clues and choose the correct words from the box.

pais	solteiros	marido	mãe

a Ele é casado; o _______ chama-se Luís.
b Eu sou filha dos (of) meus _______.
c Os amigos não são casados; são _______.
d A nossa _______ é cuidadora de idosos (*elderly careworker*).

2 A friend can't pick her aunt up at the bus station because her car broke down. She asks you to pick her up and describes the aunt to you:

> A tia Júlia é baixa, tem 73 anos, cabelos grisalhos e olhos verdes. Ela é magra, usa óculos e está com um vestido azul (*a blue dress*). Ela tem uma mala preta.

Will you be able to spot tia Júlia at the bus station? Answer True or False:

a Aunt Júlia is tall. _______
b She is wearing a hat. _______
c She wears glasses. _______
d She has a black suitcase. _______
e She has red hair. _______

3 02.08 **Numbers: listen and circle which numbers you hear.**

12 38 63 100 16 41 74 2 22 57 85 99

4 Have a go at saying these out loud in Portuguese.

a Are you married? (to a woman)
b How old are you? (sing)
c Do you have children?
d He is very tall!
e Where is he studying?

SELF CHECK

	I CAN ...
○	. . . talk about how old people are.
○	. . . talk about my family.
○	. . . express marital status.
○	. . . use numbers from 0 to 100.
○	. . . describe people.
○	. . . discuss where people are studying.

3

In this unit, you will learn how to:

» order drinks and snacks.
» express likes and dislikes.
» order a meal in a restaurant.
» discuss typical dishes and how they are served.
» ask for suggestions and recommendations.
» find your way around a Brazilian menu.

O que você recomenda?

My progress tracker

DAY / DATE					
	○	○	○	○	○
	○	○	○	○	○
	○	○	○	○	○
	○	○	○	○	○
	○	○	○	○	○

A cozinha brasileira

Brazilian cuisine is varied and has African, Indian and European influences. An enormous variety of fruits, vegetables and types of flour are used to create different dishes, not to mention the abundance of good quality meat and excellent fish. Greater African influence is found in the north-east – **muitos pratos** (*many dishes*) are made with tapioca, **carne de sol** (*Brazilian sundried meat*) and **azeite de dendê** (*palm oil*) such as **acarajé** (*black-eyed pea fritters*) and **vatapá** (*a kind of shrimp curry with a sauce made from onions, peanuts, cashews and coconut milk, and thickened with breadcrumbs*); in the north, many dishes are made with **peixes** (*fish*) found in Amazonian rivers. In the south-east and the south there is a great diversity of dishes due to the influence of those who have moved to the area. A fruit called **pequi**, native to the centre-west and north-east regions, is used a lot in the state of Goiás and in the north-east, and is eaten in dishes with rice or chicken. Also typical of Goiás is the **empadão goiano**, (*a savoury tart with a filling of chicken pieces*) and / or **linguiça** (*pork sausage*). **Feijoada** (*black bean stew with pieces of pork*) and **churrasco** (*barbecued meat*) are eaten throughout the country. The number of **vegetarianos e veganos** (vegetarians and vegans) in Brazil is growing. Therefore, some traditional dishes are being adapted and more restaurants are serving plant-based alternatives.

Self-service restaurants where you pay for your food by its weight are very popular throughout Brazil.

Can you guess what this sentence means? A feijoada da Joana é excelente!

Vocabulary builder

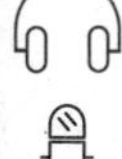

03.01 **Look at the words and phrases and complete the missing English expressions. Then listen and try to imitate the pronunciation of the speakers.**

BEBIDAS	*DRINKS*
uma cerveja	*a beer*
um chope	*a draught beer*
uma água mineral	*a _______ water*
uma garrafa de vinho tinto / branco	*a bottle of red / white _______*
um guaraná	*a guaraná* (type of plant-based soft drink)
uma caipirinha	*a caipirinha* (cocktail made from the sugar cane spirit called cachaça, lime juice, sugar and crushed ice)
um suco de maracujá	*a passion fruit juice*
uma batida	*a cocktail* (usually made from condensed milk, fruit and alcohol)
uma batida de coco	*a coconut cocktail*
um espresso	*a small black coffee*
um café com leite	*a coffee with milk*
um chá com leite	*a tea with _______*

COMIDAS	*FOOD / SNACKS*
um sanduíche de queijo / presunto / ovo	*a cheese / ham / egg _______*
um bauru	*a sandwich traditionally made using French bread, with slices of roast beef or ham, tomatoes, pickles and melted cheese*
um hambúrguer / x-búrguer	*a hamburger / cheeseburger*
uma porção de mandioca frita	*a portion of fried cassava chips*
batatas fritas	*chips, fries*
uma coxinha	*a large deep-fried chicken and potato croquette*
uma esfirra	*a Lebanese-style bread cake with minced meat filling (esfiha)*
um bolo de limão	*a lemon cake*
um sorvete de morango	*a strawberry ice cream*
um mousse de chocolate	*a _______ mousse*

NEW EXPRESSIONS

03.02 **Look at the words and expressions that are used in the following conversation. Note their meanings.**

Vamos beber alguma coisa?	*Shall we have something to drink?*
O que você quer?	*What do you want?*
Eu quero ...	*I want ...*
Não sei	*I don't know.*
Não gosto muito de cerveja	*I don't like beer very much.*
Talvez um suco	*Perhaps a fruit juice.*
Você precisa experimentar os sucos daqui	*You need to try the juices here.*
São muito gostosos!	*They're very delicious / tasty!*
O que você sugere então?	*What do you suggest then?*
Que tal ...?	*How / What about ...?*
E para comer?	*And to eat?*
Posso ver o cardápio?	*Can I see the menu?*
Você não deveria perder	*You shouldn't miss*
Divido com você	*I'll share with you.*
Vou pedir um bauru também	*I'm going to order a bauru as well.*
o garçom / a garçonete	*the server* (m / f)
Pois não?	*Can I help you?*

Conversation 1

03.03 *Mariana and Jorge pop into a snack bar to order drinks and a snack.*

1 What does Jorge want to drink?

Jorge	Mariana, vamos beber alguma coisa? Estou com sede.
Mariana	Tudo bem, Jorge. O que você quer?
Jorge	Eu quero um chope, e você?
Mariana	Não sei; não gosto muito de cerveja. Talvez um suco.
Jorge	Ah, sim, você precisa experimentar os sucos daqui – são muito gostosos!
Mariana	Ah é? O que você sugere então?
Jorge	Que tal um suco de maracujá, banana e limão?
Mariana	Ótimo! E para comer? Eu estou com fome. Posso ver o cardápio, Jorge?
Jorge	Aqui. Você não deveria perder a mandioca frita – é muito boa.
Mariana	Tudo bem, divido com você. Vou pedir um bauru também. E você?
Jorge	Eu quero um x-búrguer. [pause] Aqui vem o garçom.
(The server approaches).	
Garçom	Boa tarde. Pois não?
Jorge	Boa tarde. Um bauru, um x-búrguer e uma porção de mandioca frita.
Garçom	E para beber?
Mariana	Um suco de maracujá, banana e limão, e um chope. Obrigada.

LANGUAGE TIP

The letter **x** in the Portuguese alphabet is pronounced *sheesh / sheez*; a **x-búrguer** is supposed to sound like *cheeseburger*!

2 Read the conversation again and, with the help of the new expressions, answer the questions.

a What does Jorge suggest to Mariana that she should drink?

b What does Jorge say is very good?

c What time of day does the conversation take place?

3 03.04 **Now listen to the exchange with the server again, and supply Jorge and Mariana's words.**

Garçom	Boa tarde. Pois não?
Jorge	Say: *Good afternoon. A bauru, a cheeseburger and a portion of fried cassava.*
Garçom	E para beber?
Mariana	Say: *A passion fruit, banana and lemon juice, and a draught beer. Thanks.*

Saúde! / Tchin tchin!	*Cheers!*
com gelo / sem gelo	*with ice / without ice*
com gás / sem gás	*fizzy / still* (lit. *with / without gas*)

Language discovery 1

1 **Which Portuguese verb forms mean** *you want / I want / Can I (I can)*?

2 **Jorge describes the fruit juices as muito gostosos and the fried cassava as muito boa; what is the word muito adding to the descriptions?**

3 **If não gosto means** *I don't like*, **what do you think is the expression for** *I like*?

1 THE VERBS *TO WANT / TO HAVE TO / TO BE ABLE TO* – QUERER / DEVER / PODER

Look at how these Portuguese verbs are formed in the present tense:

	eu	você	ele / ela	nós	vocês	eles / elas
querer *(to want / wish)*	**quero**	**quer**	**quer**	**queremos**	**querem**	**querem**
dever *(to have to / must)*	**devo**	**deve**	**deve**	**devemos**	**devem**	**devem**
poder *(to be able to / can)*	**posso**	**pode**	**pode**	**podemos**	**podem**	**podem**

Remember that rising intonation at the end of a statement will turn what you are saying into a question:

Ela quer um prato vegetariano. *She wants a vegetarian dish.*

Ela quer um prato vegetariano? *Does she want a vegetarian dish?*

As well as expressing a need to do something, **dever** is also used to suppose something:

Ela deve estar com sede. *She must be thirsty.*

It also means *to owe*:

Eles devem 30 reais. *They owe 30 reals.*

você deve *you must*; **você deveria** *you ought to*
você pode *you can*; **você poderia** *you could*
eu quero *I want*; **eu queria** *I would like*
It is not considered impolite to say **quero** when asking for things.

2 ADDING EXTRAS TO DESCRIPTIONS: SAYING SOMETHING IS *VERY / A LITTLE / QUITE / REALLY*

When you want to add to a description of something, either to emphasize or intensify what the item is like, you can use the following expressions:

muito	*very*	**muito bom**	*very good*
um pouco	*a little / a little bit*	**um pouco caro**	*a bit expensive*
bastante	*quite*	**bastante salgado**	*quite salty*
realmente	*really / indeed*	**realmente gostoso**	*really tasty*

The words for *good* and *bad* in Portuguese change according to the rules of masculine/ feminine and singular / plural as follows:

masc. sing.	fem. sing.	masc. pl.	fem. pl.
bom	boa	bons	boas
mau	má	maus	más

Brazilians also use the word **ruim** a lot to describe something that is *bad* or *awful*:

esta música é ruim *this song is awful*

3 EXPRESSING LIKES AND DISLIKES

gosto	*I like.*
não gosto	*I don't like.*
gosto mais de ...	*I like ... more.*
prefiro	*I prefer.*
adoro	*I adore / love.*
destesto	*I detest.*
amo	*I love.*
não suporto	*I can't stand.*

Gostar (*to like*) needs the word **de** after it when the verb is followed by the name of what you like: **gosto de vinho** *I like wine*; **gosto de dançar** *I like to dance*. In answer to someone's question, you simply use the verb form without the **de**:

Você gosta de queijo? *Do you like cheese?*
Eu gosto, sim. / Gosto. *Yes I do.*

Practice 1

1 Use a verb from the box to complete each of the sentences.

quer	devem	posso	deveria

- **a** Eu ________ experimentar?
- **b** O que você ________ beber?
- **c** Você não ________ comer mais.
- **d** Elas ________ estar com calor.

2 Supply the correct words to enhance the descriptions.

- **a** O sorvete daqui é ________ (*really*) gostoso.
- **b** A Mônica é ________ (*quite*) inteligente.
- **c** Os produtos são ________ (*a little*) caros.
- **d** Meus primos têm um cachorro (*dog*) ________ (*smart*) esperto.

3 Choose the correct form of the words for *good* and *bad*.

- **a** Estes sucos são bons / boas.
- **b** Esta é uma mau / má ideia.
- **c** Meu celular novo (*new*) é boa / bom.
- **d** Os cigarros (*cigarettes*) fazem mau / maus para a saúde (*health*).

4 03.05 **Listen to three people say what food and drink they like or dislike, and complete the table.**

	Food or drink	Likes or dislikes?
a		
b		
c		

Conversation 2

NEW EXPRESSIONS

03.06 **Look at the words and expressions that are used in the following conversation. Note their meanings.**

para começar	*for starters* (lit. *in order to start*)
para mim	*for me*
canja	*chicken broth*
uma saladinha de palmito	*a small salad of heart of palm*
picanha com feijão	*rump steak with black beans*
a especialidade da casa	*the house speciality*
Qual é o acompanhamento?	*What does it come with?* (lit. *What is the accompaniment?*)

porco grelhado	*grilled pork*
beterraba	*beetroot*
cenoura	*carrot*
uma garrafa do vinho da casa	*a bottle of the house wine*
pavê de abacaxi	*creamy biscuit tart with pineapple*
arroz doce	*rice pudding*
Sou alérgico(a) (a / ao ...)	*I'm allergic (to ...).*
Sou vegetariano(a)	*I'm a vegetarian.*

03.07 *André and Teresa order a meal in a restaurant.*

Read and listen to the conversation, then answer the questions.

1 What does André order to accompany his main course?

Garçom	Boa noite! E então?
André	Boa noite! Bom, para começar, uma canja e uma saladinha de palmito.
Garçom	Muito bem, e depois?
André	Para mim, a picanha com feijão, e uma salada de tomate. E você, Teresa? O que você quer?
Teresa	Não sei. (*to the server*) O que você recomenda?
Garçom	Bom, tem a especialidade da casa – porco grelhado. É muito bom!
Teresa	Qual é o acompanhamento?
Garçom	Vem com arroz, batatas fritas e uma salada de beterraba.
Teresa	Sou alérgica a beterraba. Pode ser cenoura?
Garçom	Sem problema. Agora, para beber?
André	Uma garrafa do vinho da casa.
Garçom	Tinto ou branco?
André	Tinto. E uma garrafa de água mineral sem gás. Obrigado.

(Later, following the main course ...)

Garçom	Vocês querem sobremesa?
Teresa	O que tem?
Garçom	Tem mousse de maracujá, pavê de abacaxi, salada de frutas e arroz doce.
Teresa	Então queria o pavê. André, o que você quer?
André	Eu divido com você – não estou com muita fome.
Garçom	Cafezinho?
André	Dois por favor, e a conta.

2 Read the conversation again and answer the following questions.

a What comes with the grilled pork?

b What kind of wine do they order?

c Which dessert does Teresa want?

DECODING A CARDÁPIO (*MENU*)

entrada	*starter*
prato principal	*main course*
sobremesa	*dessert*
bebida	*drink*
conta	*bill / check*
gorjeta	*tip*
sal / pimenta	*salt / pepper*
vinagre / azeite	*vinegar / olive oil*
molho	*sauce*
molho de churrasco / vinagrete / agridoce	*barbecue sauce / vinaigrette / sweet and sour sauce*
contém nozes	*contains nuts*
contém amendoim	*contains peanuts*

Language discovery 2

1 **Look at the expression for a bottle of the house wine (lit. a bottle of the wine of the house): uma garrafa do vinho da casa. Why do you think do and da are different?**

2 **What expression does André use to say** *I'll share with you***?**

3 **Which words in the conversation mean** *grilled / fried***?**

1 *OF, OF THE* – DE, DO, DA

The Portuguese word for *of* or *from* is **de**. When it's followed by any of the words for *the* (which you learned in Unit 2), the words combine, or contract, as follows:

de	+o	+a	+os	+as
	do	da	dos	das

uma salada de rúcula	*a rocket salad*
gosto da sopa	*I like the soup.*
uma porção das batatas	*a portion of the potatoes*

2 -IR VERBS, PRESENT TENSE: DIVIDIR *TO DIVIDE, SHARE*

Regular **-ir** ending verbs in Portuguese form the present tense as follows:

Remove the **-ir** then add these endings to the stem. Follow the example for the verb **dividir**:

eu divido	**nós dividimos**
você divide	**vocês dividem**
ele / ela divide	**eles / elas dividem**

There are fewer regular **-ir** verbs than **-ar** and **-er** ones. Many have irregular spellings in parts of the verb. However, common regular examples include: **abrir** (*to open*), **decidir** (*to decide*) and **partir** (*to depart / to break*).

3 DESCRIBING FOOD: USING MORE ADJECTIVES

Many words used to describe the way food has been cooked, prepared or presented are adjectives and you need to remember to change their endings to match (or agree with) the food item being described.

grelhado (*grilled*), **frito** (*fried*), **assado** (*roasted / baked*), **frio** (*cold*), **recheado** (*filled*), **cozido** (*boiled*) all follow the regular pattern of changing the last letter **-o** to **-a** / **-os** / **-as**.

doce (*sweet*), **picante** (*spicy*), **quente** (*hot = not cold*) don't change the final **-e** but do add an **-s** for the plurals (masculine and feminine).

The word for *raw*, **cru**, changes to **crua** in the feminine and adds an **-s** for the plurals.

carne assada (*roast meat*), **ovos recheados** (*stuffed eggs*), **camarões picantes** (*spicy shrimps*), **peixe cru** (*raw fish*)

Practice 2

1 Complete with the correct form: de / do / da / dos / das.

- **a** Uma garrafa do vinho ________ casa.
- **b** Cardápio ________ comidas vegetarianas.
- **c** Uma sopa ________ cenoura.
- **d** O preço (*price*) ________ sucos.
- **e** A conta _______ mesa 5.

2 Translate. Say your answers out loud.

- **a** I'll share with you.
- **b** I want my coffee without sugar, please.
- **c** Two beers and one still water, please.
- **d** Do you have dishes without gluten? **(pratos sem glúten)**

3 Match the correct adjective to the items of food.

a peixe	**1** assadas
b molhos	**2** crua
c batatas	**3** frito
d carne	**4** picantes

PLACES TO EAT OUT

bar	*bar / pub*
lanchonete	*snack bar / café*
restaurante	*restaurant*
churrascaria(-rodízio)	*barbecue / grill house*
padaria	*bakery (where you can often also eat)*
comida por quilo	*self-service restaurant where you pay by weight*
mercado municipal	*market*

Listen and understand

03.08 **Márcia and Guilherme are at a praça de alimentação (*food court*) of a shopping mall in Brasília. They try to decide where to eat. Find out what kind of food each one prefers. The restaurants mentioned (Marietta and Montana Grill) are Brazilian restaurant chains, found mainly in food courts of large shopping centres, but also in some city centres.**

Márcia chooses: ______________________________

Guilherme chooses: ______________________________

Reading and writing

comida mineira	*food from the state of Minas Gerais*
comida baiana	*food from the state of Bahia*
polenta	*cornmeal boiled in water into a porridge (similar to Italian polenta)*
feijão tropeiro	*'Minas Gerais style cattleman's beans' – beans, pieces of bacon, linguiça (pork sausage) and manioc flour*

1 Fill in the gaps in the text, choosing the correct word from the box.

comida	adoramos	peixe	favorito	adoro

Maiara and her husband's favourite foods:

Eu _______ comida mineira, mas o meu marido prefere _______ baiana. Meu prato _______ é polenta com feijão tropeiro e linguiça. Meu marido prefere pratos com _______ e camarão, e molhos picantes que eu não gosto. Nós dois _______ comer numa churrascaria!

2 True or false?

a Maiara does not like spicy food.

b Maiara's husband loves food from Bahia.

c Neither Maiara nor her husband likes barbecued meat.

3 03.09 **Pronunciation practice**

The following words from the conversations all had the letter combination **ão** in them: **não, são, então, limão, porção**. This sounds like a very nasal *ow* as in the English word *cow*. Try to say it as though you have a blocked nose! Listen to these words again now and repeat them, concentrating hard on sounding like the speaker.

Go further

If you visit Brazil, you must try the delicious fresh fruit juices made **em casa** (*at home*) and in **lanchonetes** (*snack bars*). Two, three or more fresh fruits are mixed in front of your eyes and the combinations are endless. The most common are:

abacaxi com hortelã	*pineapple and mint*
abacaxi com gengibre	*pineapple and ginger*
laranja com acerola	*orange and acerola berry*
açaí com banana	*açaí berry and banana*
açaí com morango e maçã	*açaí berry with strawberry and apple*

Equally delicious are the many ice creams made of different combinations of tropical fruits and nuts. The traditional chocolate, vanilla and strawberry flavours can also be found.

As for commercially-made drinks, Brazil has **guaraná** (a refreshing fizzy drink made with the Amazonian fruit **guaraná**). It competes with Coca-Cola and Pepsi and can be bought in supermarkets and restaurants. The most famous alcoholic drink is the **caipirinha** (pronounced kai-pee-REEN-yuh), a cocktail made of **cachaça** (a sugar-cane based spirit similar to white rum), lime juice, sugar and crushed ice. **Cachaça** is also known by other names, such as **pinga** and **aguardente**. Drink it in small doses!

Test yourself

1 Fill in the gaps by choosing the correct word for each sentence.

vegetarianos vegano com não glúten alérgica

- **a** Eles ________ comem porco.
- **b** O Kauã é ________.
- **c** A Isabel é ________ a camarão.
- **d** O Calebe e eu somos ________.
- **e** Eu não gosto de chá ______ leite.
- **f** O Luís só come comida sem ________.

2 03.10 **Listen to Silvana ordering a meal and note what she asks for:**

Starter:

Main meal with accompaniment:

Dessert:

Drink:

3 Complete your part of the dialogue with the server and practice saying it out loud.

Garçom	Bom dia. Pois não?
You	Say *Good morning. A caesar salad and a slice of the cheese and spinach quiche* (quiche de espinafre e queijo).
Garçom	E para beber?
You	Say *An orange and acerola juice.*

SELF CHECK

	I CAN ...
○	. . . order drinks and snacks.
○	. . . express likes and dislikes.
○	. . . order a meal in a restaurant.
○	. . . discuss typical dishes and how they are served.
○	. . . ask for suggestions and recommendations.
○	. . . find my way around a Brazilian menu.

R1 Review 1

1 Complete with the correct forms of either ser, estar or ter.

a Eu _______ brasileiro.
b Vocês não _______ filhos?
c O Kleber _______ com sede.
d Nós _______ engenheiros.
e Você _______ um cardápio?
f Onde _______ os meus óculos?

2 Which questions would you ask to get these replies? Look carefully at the verbs used in the responses.

a _______? Eu trabalho na universidade.
b _______? Não, o Fernando não come peixe.
c _______? Partimos na sexta-feira.
d _______? Sim, gosto muito de cerveja!
e _______? Não, eles não vendem queijo.

3 Translate into Portuguese. Write out your answers.

a He is tall.
b This food is very spicy.
c She has green eyes.
d The soup is cold.
e The fruit juices are delicious.
f We are vegetarians.

4 3.11 Listen to people introducing members of the family, their ages and birthdays, and complete the missing information.

a Este é o meu _______. Ele tem _______ anos. Faz **aniversário** no dia _______ de _______.
b Esta é a nossa _______. Ela tem _______ anos. Faz **aniversário** no dia _______ de _______.
c Esta é a minha _______. Ela tem _______ anos. Faz **aniversário** no dia _______ de _______.
d Este é o meu _______. Ele tem _______ anos. Faz **aniversário** no dia _______ de _______.
e Esta é a nossa _______. Ela tem _______ anos. Faz **aniversário** no dia _______ de _______.

Who is the youngest? Who is the oldest? Whose birthday is in September?

5 3.12 **Have a go at saying these words out loud, then listen to them on the audio.**

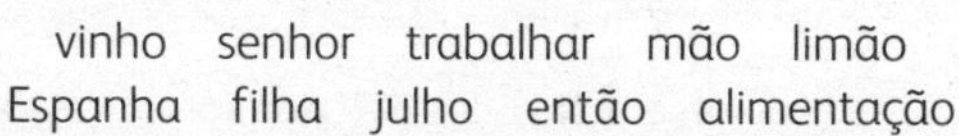
vinho senhor trabalhar mão limão
Espanha filha julho então alimentação

6 You and two friends are dining out. Look at the description of what everyone likes or dislikes, then using the menu, choose an appropriate meal for the group.

You: never have starters; don't like fish; love pork; prefer sweet puddings; like cocktails.

Samuel: prefers cold starters; allergic to seafood; likes chicken best; doesn't have a sweet tooth; always drinks beer.

Patrícia: vegetarian but can't stand tomatoes; adores ice cream; doesn't drink alcohol.

Restaurante beija-flor

Cardápio

Entradas

canja
salada de palmito
sopa de tomate

Pratos principais

camarões picantes
frango grelhado
salada César (com ou sem frango)

Especialidade da casa

ovos recheados

Sobremesas

salada de frutas
pavê de abacaxi
sorvete (variado)

Bebidas

cerveja
vinho da casa – branco / tinto
caipirinha
sucos – maracujá / açaí com maçã / laranja

	Entrada	Prato principal	Sobremesa	Bebida
You				
Samuel				
Patrícia				

7 Answer these questions out loud in Portuguese. You will find sample responses in the Answer key.

a Como vai?
b Como se chama?
c Onde trabalha?
d Você fala francês?
e Onde você mora?
f Qual é o seu email? / Tem Instagram?
g Qual é o número do seu celular?
h De onde você é?
i Você é casado(a)?
j Você tem filhos?
k Quantos anos você tem?
l Quando você faz **aniversário**?

8 3.13 **Listen to Maria and Bruno talk about themselves, and complete the missing information.**

	Where from	Nationality	Lives where	Profession / work	Marital status	Languages spoken	Phone number
Maria			São Paulo			Portuguese, French, English	
Bruno	Family from Italy				Single, but has girlfriend		

9 You are ordering a meal at a restaurant. Complete your part of the conversation with the server by following the cues.

Garçom	Boa noite! E então?
You	Say *Good evening! For starters, a carrot salad.*
Garçom	Muito bem, e depois?
You	Say *What do you recommend?*
Garçom	Bom, a especialidade da casa é feijoada. É fantástica!
You	Say *I prefer fish.*
Garçom	Então, que tal o nosso vatapá?
You	Say *OK.*
Garçom	E para beber?
You	Say *A beer.*
Garçom	Mais alguma coisa?
You	Say *And a bottle of fizzy mineral water, please.*
(Later)	
Garçom	Para sobremesa?
You	Say *A chocolate mousse, please.*
Garçom	Cafezinho?
You	Say *Yes please, and the bill / check.*

4

In this unit, you will learn how to:

» describe your habits and routines.
» talk about daily life.
» say how often you do things.
» use days of the week.
» say the words for different countries.
» distinguish between the two verbs *to know*.

A rotina diária

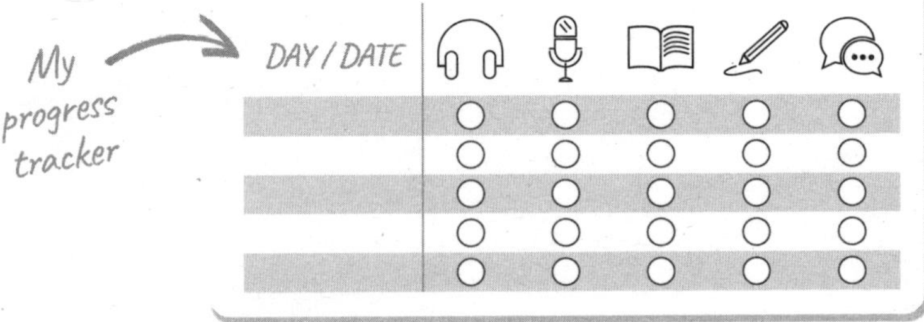

Rotinas típicas

Family life can be very hectic in Brazil, especially in the large cities, where a lot of time is spent in **engarrafamentos** (*traffic jams*) or on two or three buses, between **casa e trabalho** (*home and work*). In general, Brazilians don't eat a lot for **o café da manhã** (*breakfast*). Um **pedaço de pão** (*a piece of bread*) or **uma torrada** (*a piece of toast*) and **uma xícara de café** (*a cup of coffee*) are enough for most people. **O almoço** (*lunch*) is the main meal for most people who prefer something **mais leve** (*lighter*) in the evening, like a sandwich, rather than a heavy **jantar** (*dinner*). At lunchtime, those who work in cities tend to eat close to their office or eat a meal in the **cantina** (*canteen*) in their workplace, if they work in factories or for large companies. Lighter snacks taken during the day are often referred to as a **lanche** (*snack*), not to be confused with the English word *lunch*.

Keeping fit is important. Many like to **ir na academia** (*go to the gym*) **uma vez, duas vezes ou três vezes por semana** (*once, twice or three times a week*). At weekends many people **vão à igreja** (*go to church*), eat out and go to the **shopping** (*shopping mall*). Brazilians love to walk around large shopping malls, even if **só para ver as vitrines** (*just for window shopping*), go to the cinema or eat with family or friends at the **praça de alimentação** (*food court*).

Can you understand what Célia is saying here? De manhã, tomo uma xícara de café e como duas torradas com manteiga antes de ir para o trabalho.

Vocabulary builder

04.01 **Look at the words and phrases and complete the missing English expressions. Then listen and try to imitate the pronunciation of the speakers.**

FREQUÊNCIA	*FREQUENCY*
todos os dias	*every day* (lit. *all the days*)
o dia todo	*all day long / the whole day*
por (semana / mês / ano)	*per (week / month / year)*
cada (hora / dia)	*each, every (hour / day)*
de manhã	*in the* _______
de tarde	*in the afternoon, in the early evening*
de noite	*at* _______, *in the evening*
no fim de semana	*at the weekend*
muitas vezes	*many times, often*
poucas vezes	*rarely / seldom*
sempre	*always*
nunca / quase nunca	*never / hardly ever*
normalmente	*normally / usually*
geralmente	*generally*
raramente	_______

PAÍSES	*COUNTRIES*
a Suécia	*Sweden*
o Japão	*Japan*
a Escócia	*Scotland*
os Estados Unidos	*the USA*
a França	_______
a Espanha	*Spain*
a Inglaterra	*England*
a Alemanha	_______
África do Sul	*South Africa*
a Irlanda	*Ireland*

NEW EXPRESSIONS

04.02 Look at the words and expressions that are used in the following conversation. Note their meanings.

Você está gostando ...?	*Are you enjoying ...?*
meu horário é bastante diferente	*my timetable is quite different*
na França dou aulas	*in France I give lessons (I teach)*
até de noite	*even at night*
durante o dia	*during the day*
na minha faculdade	*in my faculty*
menos na sexta-feira	*except on a Friday*
passo uma hora lendo os jornais	*I spend an hour reading the papers.*
aí saio para conhecer novos lugares	*then I go out to get to know new places*
sei lá	*I've no idea / who knows?*
O que você acha da nossa cidade?	*What do you think of our city?*
Sinceramente, acho grande demais	*Honestly, I find it too big.*

Conversation 1

04.03 *Brazilian teacher Eduardo discusses work routines with a visiting French academic, Jean-Paul.*

1 Does Jean-Paul teach all day back home in France?

Eduardo	Então, Jean-Paul, você está gostando de São Paulo?
Jean-Paul	Sim, estou gostando, mas meu horário é bastante diferente.
Eduardo	Diferente como?
Jean-Paul	Bem, para começar, na França dou aulas só de manhã; aqui tem aulas também de tarde, e até de noite.
Eduardo	Aqui no Brasil é normal. Muitos estudantes trabalham durante o dia e estudam de noite.
Jean-Paul	Na minha faculdade em Paris trabalho vinte horas por semana. Aqui dou aulas todos os dias menos na sexta-feira.
Eduardo	O que você faz nas sextas, então?
Jean-Paul	Geralmente passo uma hora lendo os jornais; aí saio para conhecer novos lugares; sei lá – talvez tomar uma cerveja.
Eduardo	E o que você acha da nossa cidade, Jean-Paul?
Jean-Paul	Sinceramente, acho grande demais para mim, mas é interessante.

2 Read the conversation again and, with the help of the new expressions, say whether these statements are true or false.

- **a** Jean-Paul is not enjoying his visit to São Paulo.
- **b** In Brazil, Jean-Paul teaches every day except Friday.
- **c** He sometimes stops for a beer during his walks around São Paulo.

LANGUAGE TIPS

dar *to give*: **dou, dá, damos, dão**

Countries in Portuguese are either masculine or feminine, and are usually accompanied by the appropriate word for *the*: **o Brasil, a Espanha**, etc. Often, though, in the spoken language, these are left out: **Alemanha, França**. Some countries, such as Portugal, don't have the word for *the* with them at all.

grande demais	*too big* (lit. *big too much*)
caro demais	*too expensive*
longe demais	*too far*

Language discovery 1

1 Which word means *liking / enjoying* **in the following expressions?**

Você está gostando? Estou gostando

2 If na França means *in France*, **which expression in the conversation means** *in Brazil*? **Why do you think there is a difference?**

3 Which two verbs in the conversation express *knowing something* **and** *getting to know somewhere*?

1 *-ING* – EXPRESSING AN ACTION GOING ON NOW (THE PRESENT CONTINUOUS FORM)

Use the present tense of the verb **estar: estou, está, estamos, estão**, plus make the following changes to the verb of action: remove the **-ar / -er / -ir** ending and replace it with **-ando / -endo / -indo** respectively. This format is used in exactly the same way as the corresponding English, for example:

Estou trabalhando muito.	*I am working a lot.*
Mawusi está estudando sueco.	*Mawusi is studying Swedish.*

2 *IN / ON* WITH COUNTRIES AND DAYS

The word for *in* or *on* (**em**) contracts with the four words for *the* in Portuguese, becoming: **no / na / nos / nas** (*in the / on the*). The expressions are used with countries to say *in*, e.g., **nos Estados Unidos** *in the USA*, and also with days of the week to say *on*, e.g., **na sexta-feira** *on Friday*; **nos sábados** *on Saturdays*. It can also be used to mean *at* – **no fim da semana** *at the weekend*.

Sei lá	*I've no idea, who knows?*
Quem sabe?	*Who knows? / Perhaps*
Não sei	*I don't know*

3 TO KNOW

There are two verbs in Portuguese expressing knowledge: **saber**, used to express *knowing something* or *how to do something*, and **conhecer**, used to express *knowing a person or a place* and *getting to know or be acquainted with people or places*. Look out for a couple of spelling peculiarities in the present tense:

saber: sei / sabe / sabemos / sabem

conhecer: conheço / conhece / conhecemos / conhecem

Você sabe mergulhar?	*Do you know how to dive? (Can you dive?)*
Elas conhecem bem esta cidade.	*They know this city well.*

Practice 1

1 **Complete each sentence by correctly forming the parts of estar and the action word to express what people are doing.**
   a Eu (estar / aprender) _______ muito neste curso.
   b Vocês (estar / gostar) _______ da visita?
   c Eu não (estar / trabalhar) _______ esta semana.
   d Nós (estar / fazer) _______ as malas para a viagem (*to pack the suitcases*).

2 **Complete with the correct form: no / na / nos / nas / em.**
   a Nós estamos _______ praia agora.
   b _______ quintas Miguel estuda marketing.
   c Tem um bom filme no cinema _______ sábado.
   d _______ Portugal eles comem muito peixe.
   e Estou trabalhando _______ fins de semana.

3 **Match the Portuguese and English.**

a Ela conhece meu primo.	1 Does he know how to cook?
b Ele sabe cozinhar?	2 Do you know this place?
c Não sabemos a resposta.	3 She knows my cousin.
d Você conhece este lugar?	4 We don't know the answer.

Conversation 2

NEW EXPRESSIONS

04.04 Look at the words and expressions that are used in the following conversation. Note their meanings.

estamos fazendo uma pesquisa — *we're doing a survey*
Sobre o quê exatamente? — *About what exactly?*
com certeza — *OK, of course.*
eu me levanto cedo — *I get up early.*
enquanto escuto o rádio — *while I listen to the radio*
a caminho para o trabalho — *on the way to work*
certo — *right / OK*
eu vou muitas vezes à academia — *I often go to the gym.*
levanto peso e vou nadar — *I do weightlifting and I go swimming*
me divirto muito — *I have a good time, I enjoy myself.*
jantar fora — *to eat out*

04.05 *Gabriela and Sérgio are stopped in the street by someone conducting a survey on habits and routines.*

Read and listen to the conversation, then answer the questions.

1 Do the friends always have breakfast at home?

Entrevistador	Oi gente! Hoje estamos fazendo uma pesquisa – posso fazer algumas perguntas?
Gabriela	Sobre o quê exatamente?
Entrevistador	Sobre sua rotina diária, tá?
Sérgio	Tudo bem, com certeza.
Entrevistador	Legal! Então, vocês sempre tomam café da manhã?
Gabriela	Eu sim. Eu me levanto cedo todos os dias e tomo meu café enquanto escuto o rádio.
Sérgio	Eu não. Raramente como em casa. Eu bebo um cafezinho a caminho para o trabalho.
Entrevistador	E quantas horas vocês trabalham por dia?
Gabriela	Eu trabalho sete horas por dia.
Sérgio	E eu, nove, mas só de segunda a quinta-feira.
Entrevistador	Certo. Quantas vezes por semana vocês fazem exercício?
Sérgio	Eu vou muitas vezes à academia: levanto peso e vou nadar; me divirto muito, sabe? E você, Gabriela?
Gabriela	Ah, eu quase nunca faço exercício. Só na quarta-feira à noite quando gosto de correr um pouco.
Entrevistador	Finalmente, vocês gostam de jantar fora?
Sérgio	Gostamos muito, mas normalmente é só no fim da semana.
Entrevistador	Obrigado. Valeu!

2 Read the conversation again and answer the questions.

a How many hours a day does Gabriela work?
b Where does Sérgio do his exercise?
c What day of the week does Gabriela like to go running?
d How often do the friends like eating out?

AUTHENTIC EXPRESSIONS:

legal!	*great!*
valeu!	*good stuff! / okay / appreciated! / thanks!*
sabe?	*you know?*
tá?	*yes? / OK?* (from **está**)
entendeu?	*have you got that? / yes?*

Language discovery 2

1 **What do you think the 'me' means in this expression: Eu me levanto cedo?**

2 **In the conversation, find the Portuguese expression for** *I enjoy myself a lot.*

3 **What is the abbreviated expression for** *Monday* **used in the conversation?**

1 REFLEXIVE VERBS: *I GET (MYSELF) UP, I GET (MYSELF) WASHED*, **ETC.**

When someone carries out the action of a verb on themselves, the Portuguese verb comes with an additional 'reflexive' pronoun, designating the 'self' bit of the verb. These are: **me / se / nos / se**. Observe the difference here:

I wash the car **eu lavo o carro**

I wash myself (i.e., *I get washed*) **eu me lavo**

Look at the whole of the verb *to get (oneself) up* – **levantar-se**:

eu me levanto	*I get up*	**nós nos levantamos**	*we get up*
você se levanta	*you get up* (sing)	**vocês se levantam**	*you get up* (pl)
ele / ela se levanta	*he / she / it gets up*	**eles / elas se levantam**	*they get up*

You should be aware that reflexive verbs in Portuguese are not always reflexive in English. You will be able to recognize when a Portuguese verb is reflexive as, if you look it up in a dictionary, you will see that it always has **-se** after the infinitive (the verb with its full **-ar / -er / -ir** ending). Remember not to start a sentence directly with a reflexive pronoun – you need the word for *I*, *you*, etc. (the subject pronoun) first!

2 REFLEXIVE -IR VERBS WITH IRREGULAR SPELLINGS

Many **-ir** verbs often have irregular spellings in some parts of the verb, and reflexives are no different. Look at some of the common ones here, which all have a change in spelling only in the first person (*I*):

vestir-se *to get dressed*

eu me visto	**nós nos vestimos**
você se veste	**vocês se vestem**
ele / ela se veste	**eles / elas se vestem**

sentir-se *to feel*

Eu me sinto mal quando como muito.

I feel bad when I eat too much.

preocupar-se *to worry*

Eles se preocupam demais com os filhos.

They worry too much over the children.

servir-se *to serve / help oneself*

Vocês podem se servir de todos os pratos que estão na mesa.

You can help yourselves from all the dishes on the table.

3 DAYS – EXPRESSIONS AND ABBREVIATIONS

The five working days of the week can be abbreviated to **segunda**, **terça**, etc. In the written language, the expressions can be shortened even further to **2ª**, **3ª**, **4ª**, etc. and **sáb.**, **dom.**

na quarta(-feira) faço exercício	*on Wednesday I do exercise*
nas sextas gosto de nadar	*on Fridays I like to swim*
de segunda a quinta-feira	*from Monday to Thursday*
cada terça(-feira)	*each Tuesday*
todos os domingos	*every Sunday*

Practice 2

1 Complete with the correct reflexive pronoun: me / se / nos / se.

a Você ________ preocupa demais (*worry too much*).

b Eu ________ surpreendo com esta notícia. (*I'm surprised by this news*).

c Não ________ levantamos cedo nos domingos.

d Eles ________ sentem frustrados com a política. (*frustrated with politics*).

2 Fill in the gaps in the text with the correct reflexive pronoun.

As crianças ________ divertem muito na praia, mas nós ________ preocupamos quando elas ________ aproximam da água.

3 04.06 **Listen to Laura describing three of the activities she does during the week, and complete the diary using the expressions in the box.**

correer na praia trabalhar visitar amigos
jantar fora fazer compras (*do the shopping*)

Activity	2ª	3ª	4ª	5ª	6ª	sáb.	dom.
a							
	estudar						
b							
c							
		ver televisão	cozinhar				

Reading and writing

1 O que ele / ela está fazendo? What is he / she doing? Write out your answers.

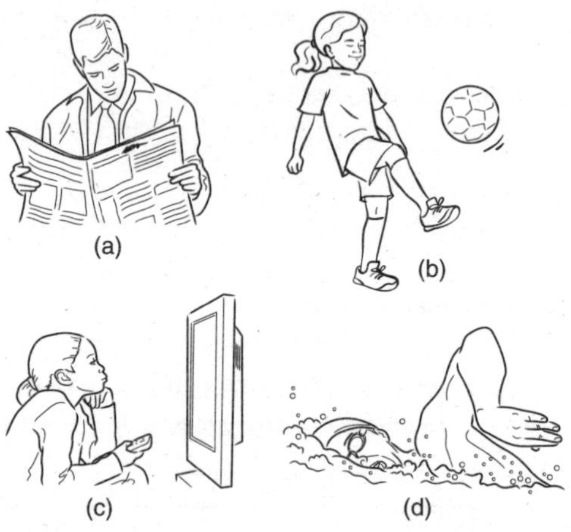

2 Here is a postcard that Samuel wrote to his family back in Brazil. Put each verb into the correct form in Portuguese (equivalent to the *-ing* form in English):

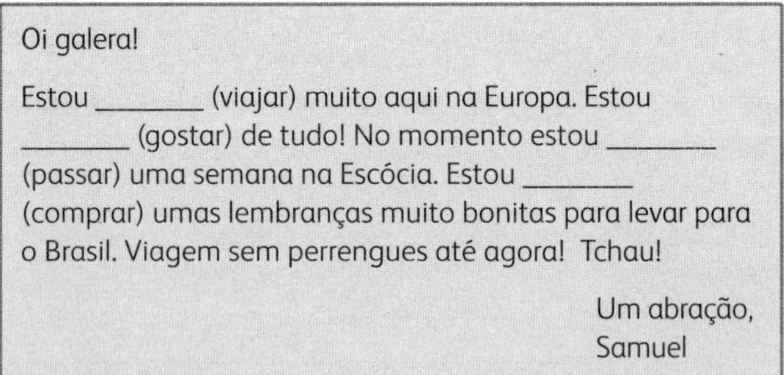

Oi galera!

Estou _______ (viajar) muito aqui na Europa. Estou _______ (gostar) de tudo! No momento estou _______ (passar) uma semana na Escócia. Estou _______ (comprar) umas lembranças muito bonitas para levar para o Brasil. Viagem sem perrengues até agora! Tchau!

Um abração,
Samuel

Oi galera!	*Hi guys! / Hi folks! / Hi everyone!*
lembranças	*souvenirs*
um abração	*lots of love* (lit. *a big hug*)
a Escócia	*Scotland*
perrengue(s) (slang)	*unexpected trouble, great difficulties*

3 Fill in each gap with the correct verb from the box.

estamos gastando (*spending*) está comendo estão vendo estou passando estamos visitando

a Eu ________ três dias em Foz do Iguaçu.
b Nós ________ muitas atrações (*attractions*).
c O Kwasi e eu ________ muito dinheiro!
d O Ricardo ________ muito churrasco!
e Vocês ________ as fotos no Facebook e os meus vídeos no Instagram?

4 04.07 Pronunciation practice

The following words from the conversations (and many others) all have the letter combination **te**: **bastante**, **diferente**, **noite**, **estudante**, **durante**, **geralmente**. The most common Brazilian pronunciation of this is **tche**, like the *ch* in the English word *church*. You'll hear this particularly in Rio. In parts of southern Brazil and the north-east, the sound is a softer **tuh** sound. Listen to these words again now and repeat them, concentrating hard on sounding like the speaker.

Listen and understand

04.08 Listen to Ana speaking about her routine, and answer the questions.

a What does Ana do every day?
b When does she go to the market?
c When does her son have English lessons?
d When does her daughter have ballet lessons?
e Where do the children have lunch every day?

Go further

Can you understand the following text? Try to get the gist of what it is about, or if you feel confident, have a go at translating it into English.

Eduardo Guedes é um chefe de cozinha famoso no Brasil. Ele é de São Paulo. Ele apresenta um programa de culinária num canal de televisão, de segunda a sexta-feira. Às vezes ele sai do estúdio e viaja para várias partes do Brasil, preparando pratos deliciosos de estados e regiões diferentes. Podemos ver as receitas e os vídeos na internet.

cozinha	*kitchen*
canal de televisão	*TV channel*
receita(s)	*recipe(s)*

Test yourself

1 Unscramble the names of the countries.

- **a** RGPUOALT
- **b** PHSANEA
- **c** ICAHN
- **d** NÁAADC
- **e** AANRÇF

2 04.09 **Listen and work out which activity each person is describing and indicate how often they do it.**

- **a** Rosana:
  trabalhar / dar aulas de inglês
  35 horas por semana / 25 horas por mês
- **b** Antônio:
  ver novelas / ir na academia
  muitas vezes / poucas vezes
- **c** Susana:
  comer o almoço / preparar o café da manhã
  sempre / geralmente não
- **d** Miguel:
  ir à igreja / ir ao cinema
  todos os domingos / de tarde

3 Have a go at saying these out loud in Portuguese.

- **a** I work 30 hours a week.
- **b** On Fridays I eat out.
- **c** I get up early.
- **d** I always do exercise on Saturdays.

SELF CHECK

	I CAN ...
●	. . . describe my habits and routines.
●	. . . talk about daily life.
●	. . . say how often I do things.
●	. . . use days of the week.
●	. . . say the words for different countries.
●	. . . distinguish between the two verbs *to know*.

5

In this unit, you will learn how to:

» ask for, and check, travel information.

» buy tickets and specify seating.

» understand numbers from 101 to 1,000.

» check prices.

» ask and tell the time.

Tem ônibus para ...?

My progress tracker

DAY / DATE	Listening	Speaking	Reading	Writing	Conversation
	○	○	○	○	○
	○	○	○	○	○
	○	○	○	○	○
	○	○	○	○	○
	○	○	○	○	○
	○	○	○	○	○
	○	○	○	○	○

Transportes no Brasil

Trens (*trains*) in Brazil are mostly **para carga** (*for cargo*), carrying minerals and grain from their areas of production to **os portos** (*the ports*). There are a few short lines for tourism only. Most transport is **por estrada** (*by road*) and some interstate coach journeys can last for more than 30 hours. An **ônibus convencional** (*standard bus / coach*) doesn't always have air conditioning, but does have a toilet, an **ônibus executivo** has reclining seats with more leg room, plus air conditioning, and an **ônibus leito** has air conditioning and seats that recline to become a bed, so you can sleep comfortably. On long journeys, the buses stop every few hours, and passengers need to pay attention when the **motorista** (*driver*) announces stopping times, such as **'tempo da parada: 20 minutos'** (*stopping for 20 minutes*).

Traveling **de avião** (*by plane*) has become accessible to many Brazilians so more people can afford to fly. In the Amazon region, **barcos e barcas** (*boats and ferries*) cross the many rivers and in some areas these are the only means of transport. In the big cities you can travel **de metrô** (*by underground*). Driving can be a nightmare for tourists as road maintenance and signaling are not always good, except on **estradas com pedágio** (*toll roads*), which are usually in good condition.

What is the driver telling you? Tempo da parada: vinte e cinco minutos.

Vocabulary builder

05.01 Look at the words and phrases and complete the missing English expressions. Then listen and try to imitate the pronunciation of the speakers.

INFORMAÇÕES DE VIAGEM	*TRAVEL INFORMATION*
uma passagem de ida	*a single ticket*
2 / 3 / 4 passagens	*two / three / four tickets*
uma passagem de ida e volta	*a return ________*
um bilhete de metrô	*an underground ticket*
a carteira de estudante	*________ card*
a carteira de identidade	*identity card*
um horário	*a timetable*
a parada	*bus / coach stop*
a plataforma	*platform*
a estação	*station*
a rodoviária	*bus / coach station, terminus*
a linha	*line (for trains or on the underground)*
o próximo ...	*the next ...*
o último ...	*the ________ ...*
atrasado	*late*

OS NÚMEROS DE 101 A 1000	*NUMBERS FROM 101 TO 1,000*
cento e um / uma	*101*
duzentos	*200*
trezentos	*300*
quatrocentos	*400*
quinhentos	*500*
seiscentos	*600*
setecentos	*700*
oitocentos	*800*
novecentos	*900*
mil	*1,000*

NEW EXPRESSIONS

05.02 Look at the words and expressions that are used in the following conversation. Note their meanings.

Quanto tempo demora a viagem?	*How long does the journey take?*
mais ou menos	*more or less*
A que horas parte?	*At what time does it depart / leave?*
A que horas chega?	*At what time does it arrive?*
oito e meia da noite	*half-past eight in the evening / at night*
É direto?	*Is it direct?*
você não tem que mudar	*you don't have to change*
Convencional ou executivo?	*Standard or executive (class)?*
um lugar na janela	*a seat by the window*
se possível	*if possible*
Quanto é?	*How much is it?*
O ônibus sai	*The bus leaves.*

Conversation 1

05.03 *Camila is at the bus terminus in Curitiba, enquiring about long-distance buses to Foz do Iguaçu so she can visit the famous waterfalls.*

1 How long does the journey take?

Camila	Boa tarde! Tem ônibus para Foz do Iguaçu?
Empregado *(ticket clerk)*	Tem, sim, todos os dias menos no domingo.
Camila	Ótimo! Quanto tempo demora a viagem?
Empregado	Demora mais ou menos nove horas.
Camila	A que horas parte?
Empregado	Parte às onze e quarenta e cinco.
Camila	E a que horas chega em Foz?
Empregado	Chega às vinte e trinta.
Camila	Tá. Oito e meia da noite. Tudo bem. É direto?
Empregado	É, sim – você não tem que mudar.
Camila	Muito bem, então, uma passagem de ida para amanhã e a de volta para sábado, por favor.
Empregado	Convencional ou executivo?
Camila	Convencional, mas um lugar na janela, se possível. Quanto é com carteira de estudante?

Empregado	São duzentos e cinquenta reais.
Camila	Aqui está!
Empregado	Obrigado. O ônibus sai da plataforma número dezoito.

2 Read the conversation again and, with the help of the new expressions, answer the questions.

a At what time does the bus arrive in Foz?

b When does Camila wish to return?

c What type of discount travel card does Camila have?

3 Now listen to the conversation again, repeating after each line, and concentrating on your pronunciation.

LANGUAGE TIPS

Quanto é?	*How much is it?*
Quanto custa?	*How much does it cost?*
Qual é o preço?	*What is the price?*

Tem ônibus? is the same as **Há ônibus?** – **há** means *there is / there are*. Many Brazilians, however, use **tem** instead of **há**.

To express means of travel (*by / on*), use **de** before **carro** / **automóvel** (*car*), **bicicleta** (*bicycle*), **ônibus**, **trem**, **avião**, **metrô**, etc., but **a** before **cavalo** (*horse*) or **pé** (*foot*).

Language discovery 1

1 **If A que horas parte / sai? means** *At what time does it leave?***, which expression in A que horas chega? means** *At what time***?**

2 **Which two different expressions both mean** *eight o'clock at night***?**

3 **The price of the ticket was duzentos e cinquenta reais (R$250); can you work out how to say** *275***?**

1 A QUE HORAS ...? *AT WHAT TIME ...?*

Use **A que horas ...?** (lit. *At what hours ...?*) whenever you are asking at what time something happens. Notice the word order: **a que horas parte / sai o ônibus para Recife?** (*At what time leaves the bus for Recife? = At what time does the bus for Recife leave?*). The English word *does* is not translated. You can make use of the following verbs, amongst others: **partir** *to depart*; **chegar** *to arrive*; **começar** *to begin*; **terminar / acabar** *to end / finish*; **abrir** *to open*; **fechar** *to close*. **A que horas abre o banco? A que horas termina o filme?**

2 EXPRESSING *AT* WITH TIME

Portuguese uses **à** (*at*) with one o'clock and midnight (**meia-noite**), **às** with all hours above one (hours are feminine) and **ao** with midday (**meio-dia**). Minutes past the hour are added on with the word for *and*, **e**, and time to the hour is expressed by **para** *to the hour*.

à uma e dez	*at ten past one*
às duas e quinze	*at 2:15*
à meia-noite e vinte	*at twenty past midnight*
ao meio-dia e meia	*at half past midday*
às cinco para as oito	*at five to eight*

24-hour clock:

dez e quarenta e cinco	**10:45**
vinte e uma e trinta	**21:30**

3 FORMING NUMBERS BETWEEN 100 AND 1,000

Before you start, refresh your memory on the previous set of numbers by going back over them a few times first. Remember that a round *100* = **cem**, but as soon as you creep over the 100 mark, the word becomes **cento** (and you never say **um cento**). The formation sequence uses **e** (*and*) between hundreds, tens and, where necessary, single units:

105	**cento e cinco**
168	**cento e sessenta e oito**
456	**quatrocentos e cinquenta e seis**

Numbers in the hundreds can have a feminine version, if you are counting feminine items:

200 towns	**duzentas cidades**

Can you understand this sentence?

Tenho três casas, trinta contas e trezentos problemas! ('problema' ends in 'a' but it is a masculine word!)

Practice 1

1 Complete each sentence by choosing a verb from the first list and a word from the second list.

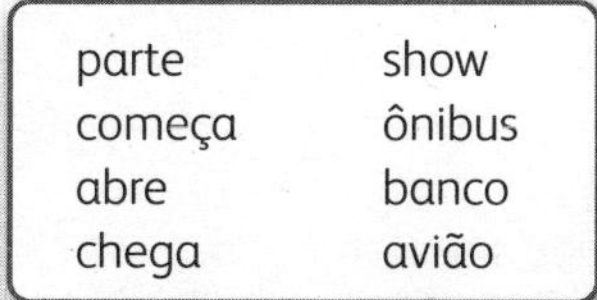

parte	show
começa	ônibus
abre	banco
chega	avião

a A que horas _______ o _______ de jazz?
b A que horas _______ o _______ leito em Brasília?
c A que horas _______ o _______ para Washington?
d A que horas _______ o _______ do Brasil?

2 What time is it? Follow the example:

Oito e vinte e cinco ⟶ 8:25
a sete e cinquenta ⟶ _______
b onze e meia ⟶ _______
c vinte para as duas ⟶ _______
d quatro e quinze ⟶ _______
e dez para as nove ⟶ _______

3 Choose the correct translation of each number.
a **126** cento e vinte e seis / cento e trinta e seis
b **491** quatrocentos e noventa e um / quinhentos e noventa e um
c **832** oitocentos e três e dois / oitocentos e trinta e dois
d **775** seiscentos e sessenta e cinco / setecentos e setenta e cinco
e **390** trezentos e noventa / trezentos e oitenta

4 05.04 Listen to the numbers and order them in sequence as you hear them.

681 232 242 599 970

Conversation 2

NEW EXPRESSIONS

05.05 Look at the words and expressions that are used in the following conversation. Note their meanings.

subir outra vez	*to go up again*
e depois descer	*and then to go down*

Com licença	*Excuse me.*
Parece que ...	*It seems / appears that ...*
Que alívio!	*What a relief! / Thank goodness!*
que horas são?	*What time is it?*
Acho que fecha	*I think that it closes.*
Chega lá rapidinho	*It gets* (lit. *arrives*) *there really quickly.*
Obrigado pela ajuda	*Thanks for the help.*

05.06 *Rafael is visiting Rio and wants to visit the Maracanã stadium (***estádio***); he needs to catch the metro to Maracanã station, so he checks with other passengers on the platform.*

1 What platform should Rafael be on?

Rafael	Por favor, sabe se esta é a plataforma certa para o Maracanã?
Senhora	Não é, não! Você precisa subir outra vez, e depois descer para a plataforma cinco.
(Five minutes later, on platform five)	
Rafael	Com licença, sabe se o trem para o Maracanã está atrasado?
Senhora	Está, sim. Olha ali no painel eletrônico. Geralmente passa um trem a cada quinze minutos.
Rafael	Que alívio! Você sabe que horas são agora?
Senhora	São vinte para as duas. Você está visitando o estádio?
Rafael	Estou. E acho que fecha às quatro e quinze.
Senhora	O trem está vindo, finalmente! Chega lá rapidinho.
Rafael	Valeu!

2 Read the conversation again and answer the statements with True or False.

a The train is late.
b There are metro trains every quarter of an hour.
c It's now twenty past two.
d The stadium closes at 16:15.
e The woman warns it takes a long time to get there.

a cada XX minutos / horas = de XX em XX minutos / horas *every XX minutes / hours*

Language discovery 2

1 **Which word is used in the text to express** *for* **or** *to* **in the following:** *for Maracanã / to platform five*?

2 **When asking and telling the time (***what time is it? / it's ...***), which of the two Portuguese verbs** *to be* **are used?**

3 **Which verb in the text means** *is coming*?

1 EXPRESSING *TO* AND *FOR*

Use **para** in expressions denoting direction *to, towards*, or *for*: **o ônibus para Fortaleza** *the bus to / for Fortaleza*; **às vinte para as cinco** *at twenty to five*; **para visitar** *(in order) to visit*; **para o aeroporto por favor** *to the airport, please* (said to a taxi driver); **para mim** *for me*.

Use **por** for expressions using *for, by / along / through, by means of*. **Por** also combines with the words for *the*: **por + o / a / os / as = pelo / pela / pelos / pelas: pelas ruas** *through the streets*; **por avião** *by air* (*by plane* = **de avião**).

obrigado(a) pelo convite / presente	*thanks for the invitation / present*
parabéns pelo aniversário / pela promoção	*congratulations on your birthday / your promotion*

2 QUE HORAS SÃO? *WHAT TIME IS IT?*

Use the Portuguese verb **ser** with time:

são X horas / é uma hora / é meio-dia, meia-noite

são duas e quinze / são oito e vinte e cinco / são dez para as seis / são doze horas

é uma e meia / é meio-dia

For clarification, add expressions such as **da manhã** *in the morning*; **da tarde** *in the afternoon / evening*; **da noite** *at night*. **São dez horas da noite. São quinze para as quatro da manhã.**

3 THE VERBS *TO COME* AND *TO GO* – VIR AND IR

	eu	você	ele/ela	nós	vocês	eles / elas
vir	venho	vem	vem	vimos	vêm	vêm
ir	vou	vai	vai	vamos	vão	vão

LANGUAGE TIP

Tickets, tickets! All Brazilians understand the word **bilhete**, but tend to use this mainly for underground tickets; use **passagem** for other travel tickets; for entry tickets to theatres and venues, use **ingresso**.

Practice 2

1 Complete with the appropriate form of por or para.

- **a** _______ mim, um guaraná.
- **b** Vamos passar _______ Belo Horizonte.
- **c** Muito obrigado _______ presente!.
- **d** Sabrina gosta de correr _______ parque (*park*).
- **e** Parabéns _______ formatura! (*graduation*).

2 Fill in the gaps with the correct form of the verb.

Lucas speaks about his routine on a normal Monday.

Na segunda-feira eu me _______ (levantar) às seis horas, me _______ (arrumar / *to get ready*), _______ (beber) um suco de laranja, depois _______ (comer) ovos mexidos e uma torrada. Por último, _______ (tomar) um café sem leite. _______ (ir) para o escritório de metrô.

3 Choose the correct form of the verbs vir / ir.

- **a** Eu vou / vai visitar minha prima.
- **b** Nós vão / vamos chegar às oito horas.
- **c** Roberta vem / vêm agora.
- **d** Os estudantes vêm / vem para a festa (*party*).
- **e** Vocês vou / vão para a praia?

Reading and speaking

1 Como ele / ela vai? Fill in the gaps with the correct form of the verb ir and the means of transport.

- **a** O João _______ para o trabalho de _______ .
- **b** Eu _______ para o parque de _______ .
- **c** Nós _______ para Salvador de _______ .
- **d** Eles _______ para a escola a _______ .
- **e** Eu e a Helena _______ para o aeroporto de Guarulhos de _______ .

(a) (b) (c) (d) (e)

2 Look at the following timetable and complete the activity.

Horário dos ônibus do Rio de Janeiro para Belo Horizonte			
Hora saída	Chegada prevista	Preço	Tipo
8:45	16:30	R$280	leito
11:00	17:30	R$150	convencional
14:45	21:45	R$280	leito
16:00	22:40	R$150	convencional

previsto(a) *scheduled*
tipo *type, kind (of bus)*

Now complete the dialogue between you and the ticket clerk at the rodoviária (*bus station*) in Rio:

You Ask *Is there a bus to Belo Horizonte in the morning?*
Clerk Sim, há um ônibus leito que sai às oito e quarenta e cinco, e um ônibus convencional que sai às onze horas.
You Ask *How much is the ônibus leito?*
Clerk São duzentos e oitenta reais, só ida.
You Say *I want two tickets for Friday morning.*
Clerk Aqui estão. São quinhentos e sessenta reais. Boa viagem!

05.07 Now practice saying your part out loud. When you feel ready, listen to the audio and try it out.

3 Que horas são? Say the correct times.

(a)

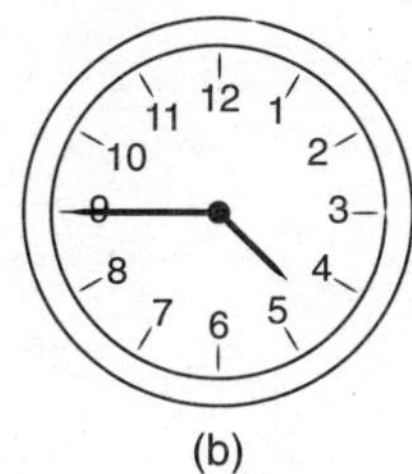

(b)

(c)

4 05.08 **Pronunciation practice**

The following words from the conversations had the letter combination **gem** in them: **viagem, passagem**. This sounds like **zhaym**: it's a soft **g (zh)** and a final **m** that's nasal in sound. Listen to these words again now, along with some additional examples, and repeat them, concentrating hard on sounding like the speaker.

Listen and understand

05.09 **Listen to Cristina describing what she has to do today and answer the questions.**

- **a** What time does Cristina have a dental appointment?
- **b** What time does she have a meeting (**reunião**) at the office (**escritório**)?
- **c** What time does she have to return home to get her suitcase (**pegar a mala**)?
- **d** What time is her flight (**voo**) to Brasília?

Go further

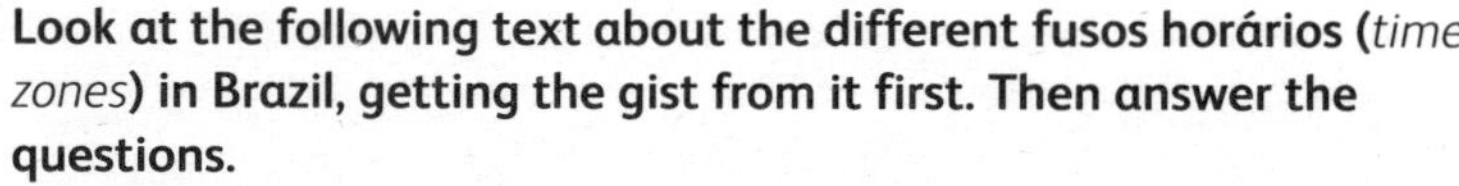

Look at the following text about the different fusos horários (*time zones*) in Brazil, getting the gist from it first. Then answer the questions.

horário de verão	*summer time*
ilha	*island*
a menos	*less*
a menos que em (Brasília)	*behind (Brasília)*

O Brasil tem quatro fusos horários. Quando é meio dia em Brasília (horário oficial), também é meio dia em todos os estados das regiões Nordeste, Sudeste e Sul, e nos estados de Goiás, Tocantins, Pará e Amapá. Na ilha de Fernando de Noronha, no Oceano Atlântico, é uma hora da tarde; em Manaus, Cuiabá e Campo Grande, que ficam a oeste de Brasília, são 11 horas da manhã – uma hora a menos que em Brasília.

No estado do Acre são 10 horas – duas horas a menos que em Brasília.

1 Complete the statements.

a Brazil has ________ time zones.

b When it is midday in Salvador, it's ________ on the island of Fernando de Noronha.

c Cuiabá, no Mato Grosso, is one hour ________ Brasília.

d São Paulo, Belo Horizonte and Florianópolis are in the ________ time zone.

2 Go back to the map of Brazil at the beginning of the course and try to answer the questions.

a O jogo de futebol começa às quatro horas da tarde no estádio do Maracanã, no Rio de Janeiro. A que horas as pessoas em Manaus devem ligar (switch on) a televisão para ver este jogo?

1 às 5 horas

2 às 4 horas

3 às 3 horas

b Dona Elza mora em São Paulo. Ela telefona para o filho, João, que está de férias em Fernando de Noronha. São nove horas da noite em São Paulo. Que horas são em Fernando de Noronha?

1 8 horas

2 9 horas

3 10 horas

Test yourself

1 Fill in the gaps with the correct word.

pegar / pode / às / no / para / da / de

Vamos chegar em São Paulo no aeroporto internacional de Guarulhos _______ 10 horas _______ manhã, _______ sábado. Você _______ nos buscar lá? Podemos _______ um Uber ou podemos ir _______ a cidade _______ trem, no Expresso Aeroporto.

2 Match the questions and answers.

a Quanto é?

b A que horas parte?

c Quanto tempo demora a viagem?

d Que horas são?

1 Parte às 18:50.

2 São dez e quinze.

3 São dez reais.

4 Demora seis horas.

3 05.10 Listen to some travel information and complete the missing details.

	destino	partida	plataforma
a	Corumbá	_______	6
b	_______	15:25	8
c	Ouro Preto	07:50	_______

SELF CHECK

	I CAN ...
○	. . . ask for, and check, travel information.
○	. . . buy tickets and specify seating.
○	. . . understand numbers from 101 to 1,000.
○	. . . check prices.
○	. . . ask and tell the time.

6

In this unit, you will learn how to:

» ask where shops and places are.
» understand basic directions and instructions.
» request further assistance.
» find your way around a Brazilian shopping centre.
» understand expressions of location.

Onde é o Hotel Recife Plaza?

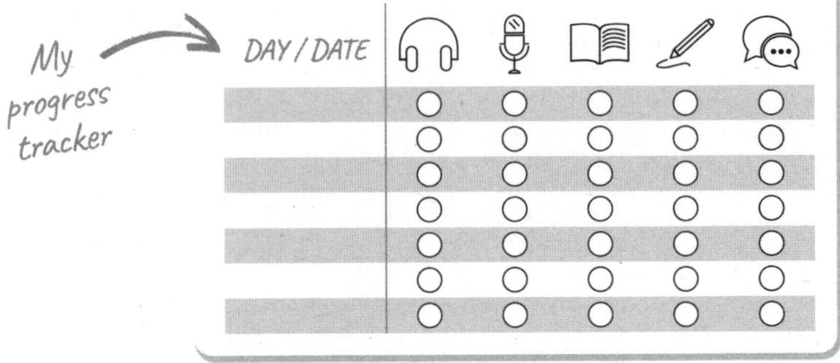

No centro da cidade

The city centers of Rio, São Paulo and Belo Horizonte tend to be **o centro financeiro e comercial** (*the financial and commercial center*), but also where old **edifícios** (*buildings*) with old-style, colonial architecture can be found, alongside modern skyscrapers. City dwellers tend to live in **apartamentos**, sometimes with 10, 15 or even 20 **andares** (*floors*). Many **prédios de apartamentos** (*apartment buildings*) have a **garagem no subsolo** (*underground garage*). Shady places with benches can be found in many parts of the cities and towns, in **parques, jardins e praças** (*parks, gardens and squares*), where it is possible to sit down, rest a while and find shade from the strong sun. It is not easy to find a parking space **no centro da cidade** (*in the city center*), **nos hospitais** (*in hospitals*) and in public service buildings, so sometimes it is less stressful to go by bus and get off at a **ponto de ônibus** (*bus stop*) near the center; some people choose to go **de táxi** (*by taxi*).

Can you understand Joaquim's address?

Avenida Cabo Frio, 250 ap. 602
Jardim Alvorada
860620-630 Londrina, PR

Check the Answer Key to see if you're right.

Vocabulary builder

06.01 **Look at the words and phrases and complete the missing English expressions. Then listen and try to imitate the pronunciation of the speakers.**

NO CENTRO DA CIDADE	*IN THE CITY CENTER*
o correio	*post office*
o supermercado	*supermarket*
o mercado	________
o hospital	*hospital*
o museu	*museum*
o centro cultural	*cultural center*
o centro de convenções	*conference* ________
a farmácia	*chemist's*
a livraria	*bookshop*
a catedral	*cathedral*
a Central de Informação Turística (CIT)	*tourist information center*
a rua	*street / road*
o jardim	*garden / small park*
o quarteirão	*block*
a esquina	*corner*
o sinal de trânsito / o semáforo	________ *lights*

DIREÇÕES	*DIRECTIONS*
à esquerda	*(to / on the) left*
à direita	*(to / on the) right*
em frente	*ahead / in* ________
perto	*near / nearby*
longe	________

lá /ali — *there /over there*
tomar, pegar — *to take*
virar — *to turn*
seguir — *to follow / to carry on*
cruzar, atravessar — *to cross*

NEW EXPRESSIONS

06.02 Look at the words and expressions that are used in the following conversation. Note their meanings.

É bastante complicado	*It's quite complicated.*
Meu Deus!	*Goodness me!*
Pode repetir um pouco mais devagar?	*Can you repeat that a little more slowly?*
É longe, né?	*It's a long way, isn't it?*
Verdade!	*It certainly is!* (lit. *True!*)
Seria melhor ...	*It would be better ...*
perguntar de novo	*to ask again*
Poderia me indicar neste mapa?	*Could you show me on this map?*
A senhora está vendo aquele sinal de trânsito?	*Can you see* (lit. *Are you seeing*) *that set of traffic lights?*

Conversation 1

06.03 *Hilary, an Australian visitor to Recife, needs help to locate her hotel, so she asks a man in the city center.*

1 Which square does Hilary have to cross?

Hilary	Desculpe! O senhor sabe onde é o Hotel Recife Plaza?
Senhor	O Hotel Recife Plaza? Bem, é bastante complicado. A senhora tem que virar aqui, à esquerda, passar pela Praça da República, cruzar a Avenida Boa Vista, e o hotel é na esquina.
Hilary	Meu Deus! Pode repetir um pouco mais devagar, por favor?
Senhor	Claro. (more slowly) A senhora vira aqui, à esquerda, passa pela Praça da República, cruza a Avenida Boa Vista, e o hotel é na esquina.
Hilary	Ufa! É longe, né?
Senhor	Verdade! Seria melhor a senhora ir até a praça e perguntar de novo.

(Fifteen minutes later, in the Praça da República ...)

Hilary Por favor! Poderia me indicar neste mapa onde é o Hotel Recife Plaza?

Senhora Sim, claro. A senhora está vendo aquele sinal de trânsito ali?

Hilary Estou, sim.

Senhora Então, precisa seguir em frente, mais ou menos cinquenta metros, e o hotel é no próximo quarteirão.

Hilary Muito obrigada!

2 Read the conversation again, and with the help of the new expressions, answer the questions.

a What is the first instruction given to Hilary?

b What does the man suggest would be better for Hilary to do?

c What does the woman ask Hilary?

3 6.04 **Now listen to the exchange with the woman again and this time supply Hilary's words. You will hear the correct version on the audio.**

Hilary *Excuse me! Could you show me on this map where the Hotel Recife Plaza is?*

Senhora Sim, claro. A senhora está vendo aquele sinal de trânsito ali?

Hilary *I am, yes.*

Senhora Então, precisa seguir em frente, mais ou menos cinquenta metros, e o hotel é no próximo quarteirão.

Hilary *Thanks very much!*

LANGUAGE TIPS

Onde é ...? *Where is ...?* and **Onde são ...?** *Where are ...?* are used for permanent fixtures, such as buildings; for anything that can move position, such as people or objects, use **Onde está ...?** and **Onde estão ...?**.

primeiro(a) *first*
segundo(a) *second*
terceiro(a) *third*
quarto(a) *fourth*
quinto(a) *fifth*

Don't forget to use the correct masculine or feminine version: **a terceira rua** *the third street*; **o quinto quarteirão** *the fifth block*.

Language discovery 1

1. **Find the expression in the dialogue that means** *(to the) left*.
2. **Find the two examples of the verb poder in the dialogue; can you guess why they are slightly different?**
3. **If vira comes from the verb virar, which verbs do passa and cruza come from?**

1 TRANSLATING *TO THE / AT THE*

The Portuguese word for *to* or *at* (sometimes even *in*) is **a**. Don't confuse it with the feminine word for *the* (which is also **a**). The *to / at* **a** combines with the four words for *the* as follows:

a	+ o	+ a	+ os	+ as
	ao	à	aos	às

ao banco *to / at the bank*

às minhas amigas *to my friends*

Don't forget all the other sets of contracted expressions, such as: **do / da** etc; **no / na**, etc; **pelo / pela**, etc!

2 REQUESTING INFORMATION: USING THE VERB PODER

Use the expression: **pode me ...?** in all kinds of situations requesting assistance:

Pode me ...? *Can you ... me?*

indicar *tell / show*

dizer *tell*

ajudar *help*

mostrar *show*

Don't forget that the form **poderia** is even more polite: *could you ...*

3 'EASY' DIRECTIONS USING THE PRESENT TENSE OF VERBS

Use the present tense of verbs, in the **você**, or polite **senhor / senhora**, format, especially to older people, to instruct people what to do:

o senhor vira à esquerda

a senhora cruza a avenida

você toma a primeira à direita

Do the same when speaking to more than one person – use the plural form of the verb:

os senhores viram aqui

as senhoras cruzam o jardim

vocês tomam a segunda rua

Practice 1

1 **Complete with ao / à / aos / às.**
   - **a** Eu preciso ir ________ farmácia.
   - **b** Manuel vai ________ supermercados.
   - **c** Pamela quer ir ________ praias.
   - **d** Nós vamos ________ museu.

2 **Translate – use você in each case.**
   - **a** Can you show me on the map?
   - **b** Can you repeat, please?
   - **c** Could you bring (**trazer**) me the menu?
   - **d** Can you help me?

3 **Unscramble the words to form questions.**
   - **a** cidade / tem / aqui / na / Uber?
   - **b** fazer / a / posso / online / reserva?
   - **c** fazer / pelo / site / posso / a / reserva?
   - **d** comida / entregam / em / casa / a / vocês?

4 06.05 **Listen to someone asking for help, and place the directions in the order you hear them.**
   - **a** turn right
   - **b** cross Augusta avenue
   - **c** go / carry on straight ahead

LANGUAGE TIPS

Some verbs relating to directions have occasional irregular spellings. Note the following:

seguir *(to follow /carry on)* ⟶ **eu sigo**, but **você segue,** etc.

subir *(to go up)* ⟶ **eu subo**, but **você sobe,** etc.

descer *(to go down)* ⟶ **eu desço**, but **você desce,** etc.

Conversation 2

NEW EXPRESSIONS

06.06 Look at the words and expressions that are used in the following conversation. Note their meanings.

devolver estes sapatos	*to return these shoes*
É neste andar?	*Is it on this floor?*
sacar dinheiro	*to withdraw / get money*
um caixa automático	*a cash machine, an ATM*
Pergunte àquela moça.	*Ask that girl.*
Pronto! Chegou.	*There you are!* (lit. *You've arrived*)
a escada rolante	*escalator*
ao lado da livraria	*next to the bookshop*
dublado	*dubbed* (into Portuguese)
com legenda	*with subtitles* (in Portuguese)

06.07 *Daniel and his friend, Fátima, meet up at the local shopping center.* **Read and listen to the conversation, then answer the questions.**

1 Which floor is the shoe shop on?

Daniel	Oi, Fátima, tudo bem? Onde vamos primeiro?
Fátima	Oi Daniel. Primeiro preciso devolver estes sapatos na Sapataria Arezo.
Daniel	É neste andar?
Fátima	Não. É no segundo andar. O que você quer fazer?
Daniel	Primeiro, quero tirar dinheiro. Onde tem um caixa automático aqui dentro?
Fátima	Não tenho certeza. Pergunte àquela moça.
Daniel	Desculpe, você sabe onde tem um caixa automático?
Moça	Vira aqui à direita, passa em frente da escada rolante e pronto, chegou! É ao lado da livraria.
Daniel	Então, eu viro à esquerda ....
Moça	Não, à esquerda, não. Vire à direita, e logo vai ver a escada rolante e a livraria.
Daniel	Então, tá, obrigado. Depois vamos lá no cinema ver que filmes estão passando.
Fátima	Boa idéia! Detesto filme dublado, viu? Gosto de praticar o meu inglês! Vamos ver se tem filmes com legenda.

2 Read the conversation again and answer the following questions:

a Does Fátima know where there's a cash machine?

b What is the cash machine next to?

c What else does Daniel suggest they do?

LANGUAGE TIPS

6th–10th: **sexto(a)**, **sétimo(a)**, **oitavo(a)**, **nono(a)**, **décimo(a)**. All ordinal numbers can be abbreviated thus: **1˚** (m.) / **1ª** (f.), **8˚** / **8ª**, etc.

To find out where the toilets are in a shopping center, ask **Onde é o banheiro?**

Language discovery 2

1 **If em means *in*, and este means *this*, can you find the single word in a contracted form in the dialogue which means *in this*?**

2 **In the instruction to Daniel to vire à direita, what is different about the word vire compared with how it was used in the first dialogue? Can you guess why?**

3 **What do the contracted expressions ao and da mean in the location of the cash machine – ao lado da livraria?**

4 **What is the word for escalator?**

1 *IN / ON THIS* OR *THAT*

The word **em** (*in / on*) combines with the words for *this* (**este / esta**) and *that* (**aquele / aquela**), and their plurals as follows:

masc. sing.	fem. sing.	masc. pl.	fem. pl.
neste	**nesta**	**nestes**	**nestas**
naquele	**naquela**	**naqueles**	**naquelas**

nesta loja — *in this shop*

naquele lugar — *in that place*

naquelas paredes — *on those walls*

2 ORDERING PEOPLE TO DO THINGS – IMPERATIVES!

To directly order people to do something (or not to do something), look at what changes from the ordinary present tense of the verb to make it a direct command:

virar *to turn* — **você vira** *you turn* — **vire!** *turn!*

All regular **-ar** verbs follow this same pattern.

Look at what happens to a regular **-er** or **-ir** verb:

comer *to eat*	**você come** *you eat*	**não coma!** *don't eat!*
abrir *to open*	**você abre** *you open*	**abra!** *open!*

The verb *to go*, **ir**, is as follows:

você vai *you go* **vá!** *go!*

Be aware, however, that many Brazilians tend to opt for the ordinary present tense version, especially in the spoken language. When listening for directions, just be alert to either variation.

3 EXPRESSING LOCATION: *NEXT TO, BEHIND, ON TOP,* ETC.

Common expressions of location include the following:

antes (de)	*before*
ao lado (de)	*next to / by the side of*
até	*up to*
atrás (de)	*behind*
debaixo (de)	*underneath / below*
dentro (de)	*inside*
depois (de)	*after*
em cima (de)	*on top of, above*
em frente (de)	*in front of / opposite*

In each case, the **de** will combine with relevant words following the expression:

ao lado do banco	*next to the bank*
em cima desta mesa	*on top of this table*
até o fim daquela rua	*up to the end of that road*
o jardim é depois da sapataria? Não, é antes.	*Is the garden after the shoe shop? No, it's before.*

4 ADDING -INHO TO CHANGE WORDS

Words can change their meaning or emphasis by altering the ending to **-inho(a)** or **-zinho(a)**. It often makes the expressions softer, smaller, or cuter:

uma casa → **uma casinha**	*a little house*
meu irmão → **meu irmãozinho**	*my little brother*
uma cerveja → **uma cervejinha**	*a nice little beer*
bonito → **bonitinho**	*really cute / nice-looking*

Practice 2

1 Complete the text according to the cues.

(In this) **a** _______ cidade, tem muitos lugares para visitar. No centro, *(in these)* **b** _______ ruas, tem bares e restaurantes. *(In that)* **c** _______ praça, tem o Teatro Municipal, e *(in those)* **d** _______ parques você pode relaxar na sombra *(in the shade)*. É muito agradável *(pleasant)*.

2 Correct each statement with an instruction. Follow the example.

Então, eu viro à direita. ⟶ Não, vire à esquerda!

a Então, eu tomo a primeira rua. ⟶ Não, _______ a segunda rua!
b Então, eu passo por aqui. ⟶ Não, _______ ali!
c Então, eu vou pela praça. ⟶ Não, _______ pelo jardim!
d Então, eu atravesso antes da esquina. ⟶ Não, _______ depois!

3 Give the diminutive form of the word. Follow the example:

A small cat ⟶ *um gatinho*

a a small shop ⟶ _______
b a small bar ⟶ _______
c a small town ⟶ _______
d a small black coffee ⟶ _______

4 06.08 **Listen to the description of where places are and indicate on the map what is located at (a), (b), and (c).**

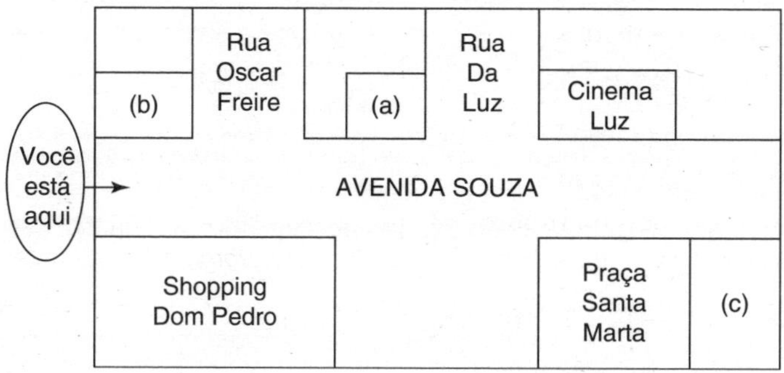

Listen and understand

06.09 Your Brazilian friend sends you a text message (uma mensagem or SMS) with instructions of how to get to her apartment. Listen to the instructions and answer the questions.

- **a** When should you get off the bus?
- **b** What should you do soon after getting off the bus?
- **c** Should you turn left or right to go to Rua Princesa Isabel?
- **d** What is the number of the building?
- **e** What is the number of the apartment?

Writing

1 You reply to your friend's message. Choose the correct word for each gap in the text.

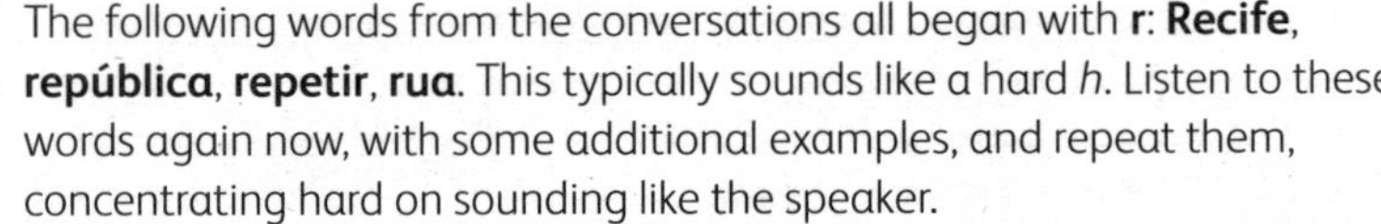

chegar horas leva antes ponto

São cinco _______ agora. Estou no _______ de ônibus. A viagem _______ meia hora. Vou _______ na sua casa _______ das seis.

2 06.10 Pronunciation practice

The following words from the conversations all began with **r**: **Recife**, **república**, **repetir**, **rua**. This typically sounds like a hard *h*. Listen to these words again now, with some additional examples, and repeat them, concentrating hard on sounding like the speaker.

Now listen to how someone from Rio (known as a **carioca**) will sound the letter **r** when it appears in the middle of or at the end of a word and repeat after the speaker: **voltar**, **viajar**, **parque**, **porque**. That sounds similar to the breathy *ch* in Scottish words such as *loch*. A person from other areas such as São Paulo or Minas Gerais rolls that **r** more; listen now to how those same words sound; be alert to different pronunciations as you travel around Brazil.

Go further

In banks, post offices, supermarkets, shops and government services buildings you will see a sign for a separate queue, where people with disabilities or reduced mobility, the elderly, pregnant women and people with babies can wait.

PRIORIDADE: PESSOAS COM DEFICIÊNCIA OU MOBILIDADE REDUZIDA, IDOSOS, GESTANTES E PESSOAS COM CRIANÇAS DE COLO.

You will find these signs inside buildings in Brazil. Can you guess their meaning?

a ***SAÍDA DE EMERGÊNCIA***

b ***ESTACIONAMENTO NO SUBSOLO***

c ***ELEVADORES***

d ***CAIXA***

e ***PROIBIDO FUMAR***

f ***ABERTO***

g ***FECHADO***

h ***RESTAURANTE NO 3° ANDAR***

Test yourself

1 Which signs do you need to look for if ...

a you're feeling hungry?

b you want to post a package?

c you need some suncream?

d you have to buy some groceries?

e you need to get some money?

1 CORREIO

2 CAIXA AUTOMÁTICO

3 LANCHONETE PAULISTA

4 FARMÁCIA LOPES

5 SUPERMERCADO

f 06.11 **Listen to the directions and complete the gaps.**

Desculpe, o senhor sabe onde é a **a** _______ Santos?

– Bem, a senhora tem que cruzar esta **b** _______, virar à **c** _______, e tomar a **d** _______ rua à esquerda. A farmácia é ao lado do **e** _______.

2 06.12 **Listen and choose the correct number:**

a é na 2ª / 6ª rua à esquerda

b é no 4° / 5° andar

c é no 7° / 9° quarteirão

d é na 1ª / 3ª praça à direita

e é na 8ª / 10ª esquina

SELF CHECK

	I CAN ...
○	... ask where shops and places are.
○	... understand basic directions and instructions.
○	... request further assistance.
○	... find my way around a Brazilian shopping center.
○	... understand expressions of location.

R2 Review 2

1 Complete with the correct form of comer, beber or conhecer.

a O Zack não ________ carne. Ele é vegetariano.
b Eu não ________ álcool.
c Nós não ________ a Amazônia.
d Eles ________ churrasco todos os sábados.
e Você ________ uma caipirinha?
f A Simone ________ muitos restaurantes em Florianópolis.

2 6.13 **Listen to Mariana speaking about her routine and answer the questions.**

a What time does she get up from Monday to Friday?
b What does she have for breakfast?
c When does she have English lessons?
d What does she do on Sundays?

3 Fill in the gaps with the correct preposition / contraction from the box.

em	no	na	de

a O aniversário do Paulo é ________ janeiro.
b Vamos nos encontrar ________ sexta-feira, ________ restaurante Pitanga?
c O churrasco vai ser ________ sábado, 10 ________ agosto.
d ________ domingo ________ tarde eles jogam vôlei ________ praia.
e Nós gostamos ________ ver as novelas ________ televisão.

4 What is each person doing? Remember to remove the final r from the infinitive of the verb and add -ndo, e.g. falando / comendo / partindo. Write out your answers.

a

b

c

d

5 6.14 **Try saying these words out loud, then listen to the correct version.**

garagem noite Rio Ronaldo passaporte porta
gente viagem bagagem azeite restaurante origem

6 You are in Rio de Janeiro and want to spend a day in Petrópolis. You go to the ticket office at the rodoviária to enquire about bus times, prices and departure times. Complete your part of the conversation using the cues provided.

You *Ask what time there is a bus to Petrópolis.*
Funcionário Há um ônibus de uma em uma hora, a partir das 8 horas da manhã.
You *Ask how much it costs.*
Funcionário 40 reais, só ida.
You *Ask how long the journey is.*
Funcionário Leva uma hora e quarenta minutos.
You *Say you want one return ticket.*
Funcionário Aqui está. Boa viagem.

7 6.15 **In Petrópolis, you want to visit the Imperial Museum. You phone the museum and listen to a recorded message about opening times and entrance fees.**

a Which day of the week is the museum closed?
b What is the charge for a student?
c What is the charge for a five-year-old child?

8 After visiting the Imperial Museum, you decide to go to the Palácio de Cristal (*Crystal Palace*). How would you ask a passerby:

a Do you know where the Palácio de Cristal is?
b Is it far?
c Can you show me it on the map?

9 6.16 **You are hungry and ask a passerby: Há um restaurante aqui perto? Listen to the answer and tick the correct instruction you need to follow.**

10 Do you remember what these signs mean? Write the correct letters next to their English translations.

a	PROIBIDO FUMAR	______	EXIT
b	SAÍDA	______	CAR PARK
c	CAIXA	______	NO SMOKING
d	ELEVADOR	______	CLOSED
e	ESTACIONAMENTO	______	CASHIER
f	FECHADO	______	LIFT

11 6.17 **Listen to the numbers and write them down.**

a ______________

b ______________

c ______________

d ______________

e ______________

12 Match the item on the left with the shop where you would buy it on the right.

a	livros	1	loja de departamentos
b	azeite	2	sapataria
c	eletrodomésticos	3	feira
d	sandálias	4	supermercado
e	frutas e verduras	5	livraria

13 You ask your friend Guilherme about his plans for the weekend. Complete the questions using a word from the box.

Onde	Quando	O que	Como	Quanto tempo

a	_______ você vai para Porto Alegre?	Vou no sábado.
b	_______ você vai?	Vou de avião.
c	_______ você vai ficar em Porto Alegre?	Três dias.
d	_______ você vai ficar?	Vou ficar no hotel Continental.
e	_______ você vai fazer lá?	Vou no casamento da minha prima.

7

In this unit, you will learn how to:

» discuss your hotel booking.
» find out about hotel facilities.
» find your way around a hotel.
» check opening and meal times.
» talk about minor problems.
» complete a typical hotel check-in form.

Temos uma reserva

My progress tracker

DAY / DATE					
	○	○	○	○	○
	○	○	○	○	○
	○	○	○	○	○
	○	○	○	○	○
	○	○	○	○	○

Alojamento

There are different kinds of **hotéis** (*hotels*) in Brazil. If you want **férias** (*holidays*) with peace and tranquility, you can chill out at a **hotel-fazenda**, generally found in the countryside and featuring large green spaces, walking tracks, horse riding and other sports facilities. There are also many eco-resorts (some self-sustainable) in regions such as the Pantanal, the Amazon and on the island of Fernando de Noronha, where you can enjoy close contact with nature as well as enjoy the many facilities of the property. **Turismo de Aventura** (*adventure tourism*) is becoming very popular, and you can try activities such as rafting or bungee-jumping nearby. Hotels and **pousadas** (*guest houses*) are classified in stars, in line with many parts of the world, **cinco estrelas** (*five stars*) being the best. The word for a room is either **quarto** or **apartamento**, the latter not necessarily being an apartment at all. In general, **café da manhã** is included in the **diária** (*daily rate*) and offers different kinds of **pão**, **bolo**, **queijo e sucos de frutas**, as well as **ovos e bacon**.

It is a good idea to discover when the **época seca e época de chuva** (*dry season and rainy season*) are in each region before you travel.

If you want to spend a few days in the countryside where you can ride a horse, which kind of accommodation would you look for in Brazil?

Vocabulary builder

07.01 **Look at the words and phrases and complete the missing English expressions. Then listen and try to imitate the pronunciation of the speakers.**

NO HOTEL	*IN THE HOTEL*
um quarto de casal	*a double room*
um quarto de solteiro	*a single room*
um quarto para família	*a _______ room*
com vista	*with view*
as refeições	*meals*
o almoço	*lunch*
a sala de reuniões	*meeting room*
acesso à internet	*internet _______*

NO QUARTO	*IN THE ROOM*
a cama	*bed*
a toalha	*towel*
o travesseiro	*pillow*
os lençóis	*sheets*
o chuveiro	*shower*
o frigobar	*minibar / fridge*
o ar-condicionado	_______
o ventilador	*fan*
o cofre	*safe deposit box*
quartos adaptados para usuários de cadeira de rodas	*rooms adapted for wheelchair users*

NEW EXPRESSIONS

07.02 **Look at the words and expressions that are used in the following conversation. Note their meanings.**

Temos uma reserva	*We have a reservation.*
Quais são os seus nomes?	*What are your names?*
Como se escreve ...?	*How do you spell ...?* (lit. *How is written ...?*)
Vocês se importam de preencher esta ficha?	*Do you mind filling in this form?*

A recepção fica aberta	*The reception stays open.*
a partir das sete e meia	*from 7.30 onwards*
de manhã cedo	*early in the morning*
de fácil acesso	*easily accessible* (lit. *of easy access*)
a praia de Encantadas é mais movimentada	*the Encantadas beach is busier*
Boa estada!	*Have a good stay!*

Conversation 1

07.03 *Edward and Susan Towers are checking into the guesthouse Pousada Baleia on the island Ilha do Mel, in southern Brazil, a place known for its ecotourism and tranquillity.*

1 How long is the room booked for?

Edward	Bom dia!
Recepcionista	Bom dia. Pois não?
Edward	Temos uma reserva; um apartamento reservado para oito noites.
Recepcionista	Quais são os seus nomes, por favor?
Edward	Edward e Susan Towers.
Recepcionista	Desculpe, mas como se escreve o seu sobrenome?
Edward	T-O-W-E-R-S: Towers
Recepcionista	Certo. Vocês se importam de preencher esta ficha, por favor? *(pause)* Vocês têm passaportes?
Susan	Aqui.
Recepcionista	Pronto! Esta é a chave do apartamento número vinte e cinco, no segundo andar; a recepção fica aberta vinte e quatro horas por dia.
Susan	A que horas servem o café da manhã?
Recepcionista	Bom, tem café a partir das sete e meia, até as nove horas.
Susan	Que legal! A gente quer ir para a praia de manhã cedo.
Recepcionista	Ah sim – as praias aqui são de fácil acesso; a praia de Fortaleza é deserta, mas a praia de Encantadas é mais movimentada. Boa estada!

2 Read the conversation again and match the questions and answers.

a Quais são os seus nomes?
b Como se escreve o seu sobrenome?

1 Aqui.
2 T-O-W-E-R-S.

c Vocês têm passaportes?
d A que horas servem o café da manhã?

3 Edward e Susan Towers.
4 Tem café a partir das sete e meia.

LANGUAGE TIPS

Vocês se importam de ... *Do you mind ...* is a more polite version of asking **Vocês poderiam ...?** *Could you ...?*:

Vocês se importam de assinar aqui / esperar um momento? *Do you mind signing here / waiting a moment?*

Describing places:

calmo	*calm*
tranquilo	*peaceful*
limpo	*clean*
poluído	*polluted*
barulhento	*noisy*

Remember to change the ending to **-a** to describe feminine places: **é uma praia limpa.**

Boa estada! / Boa estadia!	*Have a nice stay!*
Boas férias!	*Enjoy your holidays!*
Boa viagem!	*Have a good journey!*

Language discovery 1

1 **How are Edward and Susan asked to spell out their surname?**
2 **Find the plural equivalent of this question in the dialogue: Qual é o seu nome? What has changed?**
3 **Which verb is used, in its infinitive form, in the time expression from 7.30 (onwards)? What does the verb usually mean?**
4 **Which three expressions describe the beaches on the island?**

1 THE ALPHABET REVISITED

You may well be asked to spell out your name, or part of your address, whilst giving personal information; go back to the audio of the alphabet and tricky sounds from the start of this course and try hard to copy the speaker's pronunciation. Practice your own names in advance of your visit, and focus particularly on those letters which may have a less familiar sound to you.

2 IRREGULAR PLURALS: L ⟶ IS

Nouns and adjectives ending in **-l** in Portuguese form their plurals as follows:

-al remove **-l** and add **-is** ⟶ **-ais jornal** ⟶ **jornais** *newspapers*

-el remove **-l** and add **-is** ⟶ **-éis papel** ⟶ **papéis** *papers / paperwork*

-ol / -ul remove **-l** and add **-is** ⟶ **-óis / -uis lençol** ⟶ **lençóis**; **azul** ⟶ **azuis**

-il remove **-l** and add **-s** or **-eis** ⟶ **-is / -eis gentil** ⟶ **gentis** *kind*; **difícil** ⟶ **difíceis** *difficult*

Note that some are easier to construct than others depending on the sound of the original word, and may require an additional written accent. Learn them as you go along and make a note of any new ones you find, especially those requiring a written accent.

3 FROM ... UNTIL ...

A partir de ... means *from ... (onwards)*, and can be used with all manner of time expressions: **a partir das sete horas**, **a partir da sexta-feira**, **a partir de julho**, etc. To express *up to / until*, use **até**. You will also hear the simple expression **de** (or **do**, etc.) ... *from ...*: **da uma hora até as duas e trinta**, **do domingo até a terça-feira**, **de março até maio.**

4 ADJECTIVES WITH SER

Don't forget that when using the verb *to be* to describe anything fixed or permanent, use **ser**, and make your adjectives agree with what they are describing in number and gender (masculine or feminine):

as praias são lindas

o hotel é barato

você é engraçado (*funny*)

Practice 1

1 07.04 **Listen to people spelling their surnames and work out what they are.**

a ________________

b ________________

c ________________

2 Choose the correct form of each word.

- **a** O exercício não é fácil / fáceis.
- **b** Os hotel / hotéis são luxuosos (*luxury*).
- **c** Estes lençol / lençóis são de algodão (*cotton*).
- **d** Gosto muito de vinho espanhol / espanhóis.
- **e** A água é azul / azuis turquesa (*turquoise*).

3 Unscramble the words to form sentences.

- **a** abre / o restaurante / para / o almoço / ao meio dia
- **b** das / a partir / o café da manhã / seis / é servido
- **c** música / todos / tem/ ao vivo / os / sábados
- **d** fica / a cidade / o carnaval / sempre / lotada / durante

4 Fill in the gaps with the correct words.

o quarto	os apartamentos	a cidade	as praias

- **a** __________ é grande e movimentada.
- **b** __________ são lindas, mas muito cheias (*crowded*).
- **c** __________ é confortável e moderno, mas está muito sujo.
- **d** __________ são pequenos e caros.

Conversation 2

NEW EXPRESSIONS

07.05 **Look at the words and expressions that are used in the following conversation. Note their meanings.**

Desculpe incomodar	*Sorry to bother you*
acabo de chegar	*I have just arrived.*
a convenção sobre biodiversidade	*the conference about biodiversity*
Falta um livrinho de informações	*There's an information booklet missing.*
para o uso exclusivo dos nossos hóspedes	*for the exclusive use of our guests*
Aliás	*What is more / Moreover*
Quais são as horas de abertura?	*What are the opening times?*
está suja e precisamos limpar	*it's dirty and we need to clean it*
a qualquer hora	*at any time*

07.06 *Argentinian businesswoman Edith García is checking out the facilities at the hotel where her conference is being held.*

1 Which room is Edith looking for?

Edith	Boa tarde! Desculpe incomodar – acabo de chegar e queria me informar sobre as instalações do hotel.
Recepcionista	Com certeza. A senhora está aqui para a convenção sobre biodiversidade?
Edith	Estou, sim. Onde fica a sala de reuniões? Falta um livrinho de informações no quarto.
Recepcionista	Um momento, sim? *(calls to colleague)* – Marta, vou orientar a senhora García por dez minutos, tá?
Marta	Tudo bem, Francisco.
Recepcionista	(*slowly*) Então, aqui, à esquerda, tem a sala de convenções, com mais quatro salas de reuniões ao lado. Ao fim do corredor, no canto, tem escritório com computadores para o uso exclusivo dos nossos hóspedes. Aliás, todos os quartos têm acesso à internet.
Edith	Ótimo!

07.07 *The tour of the hotel continues.*

2 What are the opening times of the hotel gym?

Recepcionista	Depois, temos nossa academia no subsolo do hotel; tem piscina, jacuzzi, sauna, tudo.
Edith	Quais são as horas de abertura?
Recepcionista	Geralmente, abre a partir das seis da manhã, e fecha às vinte e três horas. Hoje a sauna está fechada porque está suja e precisamos limpar.
Edith	E a que horas são as refeições?
Recepcionista	O restaurante abre às seis e trinta para o café da manhã. Também serve almoço e jantar, mas também pode comer refeições ligeiras no bar a qualquer hora.

3 Read, then listen to, both conversations again and answer the questions.

a Is the conference room on the left or the right?

b Where is the hotel gym located?

c Why is the sauna closed today?

d When can you eat light meals in the bar?

LANGUAGE TIPS

More prepositions:

no canto	*in the corner*
ao fim de / no fim de	*at the end of*

You can express what's not working properly in your room by using **não funciona / funcionam** *it doesn't work / they don't work*:

a torneira não funciona	*the tap doesn't work*

Language discovery 2

1 **In the expression for** *I have just arrived*, **which verb means** *to arrive*? **What verb does acabo come from?**

2 **What is the word order in Portuguese for the phrase** *there's a booklet missing*?

3 **If convenções is the plural of convenção, what is the singular of reuniões?**

4 **Which two adjectives describe the current state of the hotel sauna?**

1 ACABAR DE ... *TO HAVE JUST ...*

To express an action that has just taken place, use the present tense of the verb **acabar**, followed by **de**, then the action in the infinitive form of the verb:

acabo de jantar	*I've just had dinner.*
ela acaba de partir	*she's just left*
acaba de chover	*it's just rained*

2 FALTAR *TO BE MISSING / LACKING*

Faltar could be described as a sort of back-to-front verb, as you follow it by the item or items that are missing. Use it in the third person singular or plural forms:

Falta uma toalha; **falta leite**; **faltam dois garfos** (*forks*); **faltam pratos**

You may also hear the expression **há / tem uma falta de ...** *there's a lack of ...*:

há uma falta de educação	*there's a lack of good manners*

3 IRREGULAR PLURALS: ÃO

Nouns and adjectives ending in **-ão** in Portuguese form their plurals in the following ways – but there are no hard and fast rules about which form any particular word takes; you need to learn new plurals as you come across them:

ão → **ões** (the most common) OR → **ães** → OR → **ãos**

estação → **estações** **pão** → **pães** **mão** → **mãos**

4 ADJECTIVES WITH ESTAR

When using *to be* to describe anything temporary or not fixed, such as weather, emotions, state of health, situations that can change or have changed, use the verb **estar** with adjectives, remembering to make those agree with the nouns in question:

a banheira não está limpa	*the bathtub isn't clean*
todos os museus estão fechados hoje	*all the museums are closed today*

Practice 2

1 Match the expressions to the pictures to say what has just happened.

a

b 

1 acaba de chover
2 acabam de partir
3 acabamos de jantar
4 acabo de chegar

c 

d 

2 07.08 **Listen and decide what's missing.**

a ________________
b ________________
c ________________
d ________________
e ________________

3 Find the word that doesn't match the ending pattern. Then decide what the singular of that word is.

a alemães	aviões	pães	capitães (*captains*)
b irmãos	mãos	estações	grãos (*grains*)
c porções	atrações	televisões	órgãos (*organs*)

4 Complete with the correct part of estar from the first line in the box and an appropriate adjective from the next two lines.

> estão está estou estamos tristes (*sad*)
> cansada (*tired*) abertas frio

a Eu (f.) _______ _______.
b Hoje o tempo (*weather*) _______ muito _______.
c As lojas não _______ _______ hoje.
d Nós _______ _______.

Reading and listening

William reads an advert for a hotel in Ilhabela, on the coast of the state of São Paulo.

Read the advert and answer the questions.

Hotel Itapemar em Ilhabela - rodeado por muito verde e uma paisagem linda e relaxante. Um local perfeito para passeios a pé e de bicicleta. A praia fica pertinho! São sessenta apartamentos grandes, confortáveis e bem equipados. O restaurante serve pratos deliciosos de peixe. A área de lazer inclui sauna, quadras de squash e tênis.

rodeado por	*surrounded by*
relaxante	*relaxing*
paisagem	*countryside*

1 **What is the location perfect for?**

2 **How many rooms are there?**

3 **What dishes might tempt you in the restaurant?**

4 **What leisure activities can you participate in?**

07.09 *William decides to go to Ilhabela and makes a reservation at the Hotel Itapemar. He is in the city of São Paulo at the moment.*

Listen to the dialogue and answer the questions.

balsa	*a barge or ferry that transports people and vehicles*

5 How can William get to Ilhabela from São Paulo?

a by bus or car and then on foot

b by boat and then by car

c by bus or car and then by boat

6 How long will it take to get to Ilhabela, from São Sebastião?

a 15 minutes

b half an hour

c an hour

7 How often do the barges leave for Ilhabela?

a once a day

b twice a day

c many times a day

8 07.10 **Pronunciation practice**

The word for *underground* is spelled **S-U-B-S-O-L-O**, but many Brazilians say it as though there were an **I** after the **B**. Listen to that word again now. Try picturing the spelling of the word and then its pronunciation as you say it. Other examples of where an extra vowel is often added when speaking include: **absurdo** *absurd* (sounds like **abisurdo**), **Magda** (sounds like **Máguida**) and **ritmo** *rhythm* (sounds like **ritimo**). There is further guidance on this in the **Pronunciation guide** at the start of the course.

Reading

Sonia writes a feedback form to the management of the hotel where she stayed in São Paulo:

> Este hotel precisa de uma renovação. O controle remoto da televisão não funciona. O acesso à internet não está incluído no preço da diária, uma grande inconveniência. As cortinas estão sujas e o chuveiro é ruim. Não é um hotel de três estrelas, mas de duas estrelas! Fiquei decepcionada (I was disappointed).

What does Sonia say is wrong with the room? Find the correct answer in the second column.

a remote control
b shower
c internet access
d curtains

1 dirty
2 not included in the price
3 does not work
4 rubbish

Go further

Look at the hotel check-in form that William had to fill in when he arrived in Ilhabela.

Ficha de registro de entrada no hotel	
Nome: *William*	Sobrenome: *Slater*
Data de nascimento *10/05/1963*	Local de nascimento: *York, Inglaterra*
Número da Identidade / Passaporte: *900352803*	
Endereço: *305 Whitestone Street, Kendal LA9 Inglaterra*	
E-mail: slater63@gmail.com	
Telefone celular: +44 7001123679	

data de nascimento *date of birth*
local de nascimento *place of birth*
número da identidade / passaporte *identity card / passport number*
endereço *address*

The date 10/05/1963 means day/month/year.

Now complete the form with your own details.

Ficha de registro de entrada no hotel	
Nome:	Sobrenome:
Data de nascimento:	Local de nascimento:
Número da Identidade / Passaporte:	
Endereço:	
E-mail:	
Telefone celular:	

Test yourself

1 Rearrange the words into complete sentences.

a não / chuveiro / o / funciona

b que / abre / a / bar / horas / o ?

c código / qual / do / wi-fi / é / o ?

d chamar / pode / um / nós / táxi / para ?

> o código OR a senha do wifi
> = the password for the wifi

2 07.11 Listen to the conversation and complete with the missing information in Portuguese.

a Tipo de quarto? _______

b Para quantas noites? _______

c Sobrenome? _______

d Número do quarto? _______

3 Have a go at saying these out loud in Portuguese.

a I have a reservation.

b We have a room booked for five nights.

c What time is breakfast served?

d Does the room have a safe deposit box?

SELF CHECK

	I CAN ...
○	. . . discuss my hotel booking.
○	. . . find out about hotel facilities.
○	. . . find my way around a hotel.
○	. . . check opening and meal times.
○	. . . talk about minor problems.
○	. . . complete a typical hotel check-in form.

8

In this unit, you will learn how to:

» ask for clothing and other items by color and size.
» understand and react to recommendations and suggestions.
» specify *this*, *that*, *these* and *those*.
» request information about products.
» understand numbers above 1,000.

Pois não?

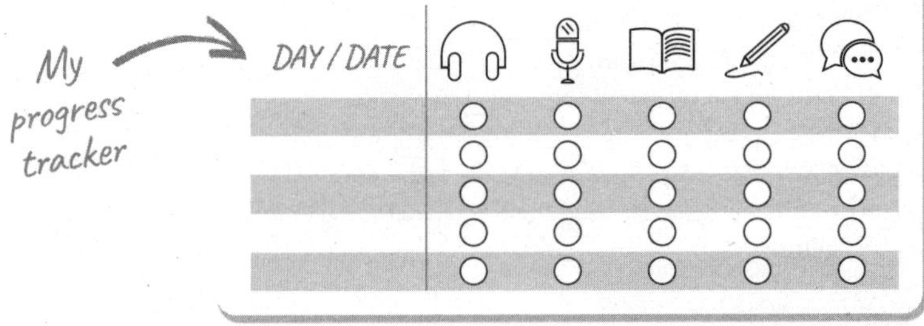

Fazendo compras

Many Brazilians like to do their weekly or monthly shopping in hypermarkets such as Extra, Carrefour, Walmart and Makro, where they can buy everything and there is **estacionamento grátis** (*free parking*). Some cities and towns have designated shopping streets with a large concentration of small shops selling all kinds of products at big discounts. Middle-class Brazilians in particular are big fans of shopping malls, referred to as **o shopping**, and also love to visit **lojas de departamentos** (*department stores*). Fun shopping can also be had at local **feirinhas** (*markets* – mostly for fresh food) and the **feira hippie** (*artisan / craft market*). If you are in search of bargains, look for signs saying **LIQUIDAÇÃO** (*sale*) and **DESCONTOS** (*discounts*). In general, you can buy **roupas** (*clothes*), **sapatos** (*shoes*) and **móveis** (*furniture*) **à vista** (*paid there and then*) or **à prazo e sem juros** (*paid in interest-free instalments*).

What does this sign mean?

LIQUIDAÇÃO 40% de desconto nas compras à vista e a prazo.

Vocabulary builder

08.01 **Look at the words and phrases and complete the missing English expressions. Then listen and try to imitate the pronunciation of the speakers.**

ROUPA(S)	*CLOTHING / CLOTHES*
a blusa	______
a saia	*skirt*
a calça	*trousers*
o vestido	*dress*
a camiseta	*T-shirt*
a camisa	*shirt*
o terno	*suit*
a gravata	*tie*
os tênis	*trainers / sneakers*
as sandálias	______
o short	*shorts*

LANGUAGE TIP

The words for *trousers* and *shorts* are singular in Portuguese. **Tênis** can also be singular when it refers to one trainer and the singular forms of **sandálias** and **sapatos** are **sandália** and **sapato** respectively.

CORES	*COLORS*
preto	*black*
branco	______
amarelo	*yellow*
vermelho	*red*
roxo	*purple*
azul	*blue*
verde	______
laranja	*orange*
marrom	*brown*
cinza	*grey*
(cor-de-)rosa	*pink*
bege	______

NEW EXPRESSIONS

08.02 **Look at the words and expressions that are used in the following conversation. Note their meanings.**

talvez de seda, com manga comprida	*perhaps (made of) silk, with short sleeves*
no tamanho	*in size*
são de linho	*they're (made of) linen*
São as mais bonitas da loja.	*They're the prettiest in the shop.*
deixe-me ver	*let me see*
temos aquelas ali	*we have those over there*
essa que você tem aí	*that one that you have there*
À vontade.	*Of course / As you wish.*
o provador	*the changing room*
combina bem	*it goes well*

Conversation 1

08.03 *Rodrigo has gone shopping with his friend Vanda, who wants a new blouse.*

1 What color of blouse is Vanda looking for?

Rodrigo	Vanda, que tipo de blusa você está procurando?
Vanda	Talvez de seda, com manga comprida, sei lá, Rodrigo, depende do preço.
(The shop assistant approaches).	
Funcionária	Pois não, senhora?
Vanda	Boa tarde. Estou procurando uma blusa preta; o que vocês têm no tamanho quarenta?
Funcionária	Bom, temos estas aqui, que são de linho – muito confortáveis.
Vanda	Quanto custam?
Funcionária	Sessenta e cinco reais cada. São as mais bonitas da loja.
Vanda	Hmm, um pouco cara para mim. Não tem mais barata?
Funcionária	Mais barata, hmm, deixe-me ver – temos aquelas ali de algodão em várias cores.
Vanda	Posso experimentar essa que você tem aí?
Funcionária	À vontade. O provador é ali, à esquerda.

(Five minutes later)

Vanda Então, Rodrigo, o que você acha?

Rodrigo Nossa Vanda, que linda! Fica muito bem em você. Acho que combina bem com a sua saia.

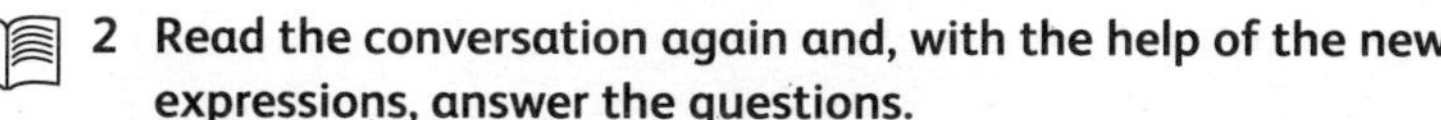

2 Read the conversation again and, with the help of the new expressions, answer the questions.

a What is the price of the linen blouses?

b Where is the changing room located?

c According to Rodrigo, what does the blouse go well with?

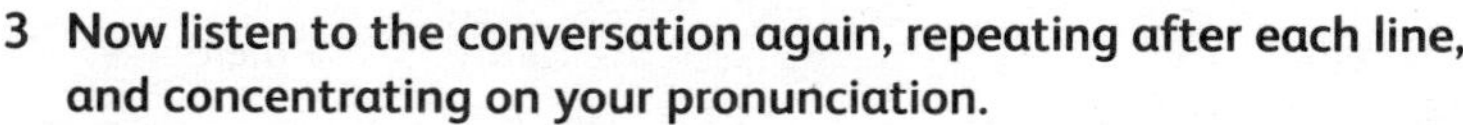

3 Now listen to the conversation again, repeating after each line, and concentrating on your pronunciation.

INSIGHT

Clothing sizes in Brazil follow European sizes, or are expressed as: **pequeno** (**P**), **médio** (**M**), **grande** (**G**) and **extra grande** (**GG**). Shoe sizes are different from European and American sizes. It's always best to try first, as Brazilian sizes can often be smaller than in the United States, in the UK and in other countries.

fica / ficam bem	*it suits / they suit you*
serve / servem	*it fits / they fit*
combina / combinam com ...	*it goes / they go with ...*
está apertado(a)	*it's tight*
manga comprida / curta	*long- / short-sleeved*
de veludo / jeans / cetim / couro / lã	*(made of) velvet / denim / satin / leather / wool*
xadrez	*checked*
listrado	*striped*
florido	*flowery*

Language discovery 1

1 Find the expression for a black blouse. How do you think you say *a white blouse***?**

2 What is the opposite of estas aqui?

3 Find the Portuguese for a) *expensive* **b)** *cheaper* **(i.e.** *more cheap***) c)** *the prettiest* **(i.e.** *the most pretty***). Why are the adjectives all feminine?**

1 ADJECTIVES OF COLOR

Colors ending in **-o** have four different forms depending on gender and number:

preto → preta / pretos / pretas

uma blusa preta

os sapatos pretos

Those ending in **-e** or a consonant only have one singular and one plural form:

verde → verdes **azul → azuis** **marrom → marrons**

uma camisa azul

meias (*socks*) **marrons**

Colors such as **cinza**, **laranja** and **(cor-de-)rosa** don't change at all:

um biquíni laranja

os maiôs (*swimming costumes*) **cor-de-rosa**

If you're unsure, you can express a colour in its masculine singular form, preceding it by **em** (*in*):

uma sunga (*swimming trunks*) **cinza**

You can also use **-escuro** (*dark*) and **-claro** (*light*):

uma saia verde-escura

um chapéu (*hat*) **roxo-claro**

2 *THIS* AND *THAT*; *HERE* AND *THERE*

	masc. sing.	masc. pl.	fem. sing.	fem. pl.	
aqui (*here*)	**este**	**estes**	**esta**	**estas**	*this / these*
aí (*there*)	**esse**	**esses**	**essa**	**essas**	*that / those*
ali (*over there*)	**aquele**	**aqueles**	**aquela**	**aquelas**	*that / those*

You should use **esse**, etc. when referring to something near to the person you're talking to (i.e. that thing you have there). For anything at a distance from both parties, use **aquele**, etc.

O tecido desta blusa é bom, mas o tecido daquela ali é muito melhor. — *The fabric of this blouse is good, but the fabric of that one is much better.*

Aquelas camisas são as minhas favoritas e estão na oferta. — *Those shirts are my favourites and they are on offer.*

In practice, however, Brazilians don't pay much attention to the rules! You will come across **aí** and **ali** used interchangeably as well as **lá** for *over there*, far from the speaker. Be prepared for anything!

3 CHEAP, CHEAPER, CHEAPEST

To compare things using adjectives, use **mais** (*more*) and the correct form of the adjective: **esta calça é mais barata** *these trousers are cheaper* (lit. *more cheap*); to express the extreme, or superlative, form of an adjective, place the relevant word for *the* in front of **mais**: **são os mais confortáveis** (*they are the most comfortable*). Note the following word order: **é a jaqueta mais cara da loja**: *it's the most expensive jacket in the shop* (lit. *it's the jacket more expensive of the shop*).

Practice 1

1 **Write the color in Portuguese, matching the noun's gender and number.**

Example: cinco saias (*black*) <u>**pretas**</u>

- **a** um casaco (*green*)
- **b** três camisas (*yellow*)
- **c** duas sandálias (*brown*)
- **d** uma bolsa (*purple*)

2 **Express what is in the images using** *this* **and** *that*, **etc., and** *here* **and** *there*, **following this example:**

(a)  (b)

(c)  (d)

relógio	*watch*
cinto	*belt*

3 08.04 **Listen and complete with the missing expressions.**

fresca o mais nova mais

Eu gosto muito de roupa ________. No verão uso roupa de algodão, que é mais ________. No inverno (*in winter*), prefiro roupa ________ quente; adoro meu vestido de lã – é ________ lindo que tenho!

Conversation 2

NEW EXPRESSIONS

08.05 Look at the words and expressions that are used in the following conversation. Note their meanings.

né?	*aren't they? / isn't it? / eh?*
Tem as havaianas em promoção.	*The flip-flops havaianas* (famous Brazilian fip-flop brand) *are on special offer.*
Vou levar um par.	*I'm going to take a pair.*
Combina melhor com a sua bolsa!	*It goes better with your bag!*
Estão na moda.	*They're in fashion.*
Me dá essa listrada.	*Give me that striped one.*
Estou à procura de ...	*I'm looking for ...*
música sertaneja	*country music*
Estão todos na oferta	*They're all on offer.*
O que é isso?	*What's that?*
A variedade é enorme.	*There is a huge variety* (lit. *The variety is huge*).
o mais vendido do verão	*the bestseller of the summer* (lit. *the most sold of the summer*)
já venderam	*they've already sold*

08.06 *Lara is chatting with a stallholder at the feira hippie in Natal.*

1 What does Lara buy a pair of, and in what color?

Lara	Oi, tudo bem? Que coisas mais bonitas você tem!
Vendedor	São lindíssimas, né? Hoje, menina, tem as havaianas em promoção - olha que desenhos maravilhosos!
Lara	Gosto muito destas aqui em laranja e azul. Vou levar um par – número trinta e seis, por favor. Ah, você também tem toalhas de praia, ótimo!
Vendedor	Que tal aquela? Combina melhor com a sua bolsa!
Lara	Tudo bem. Que mais você tem?
Vendedor	Estas bandanas estão na moda no momento.
Lara	Me dá essa listrada que você tem aí. Obrigada.

Meanwhile, David has come across a stall selling second-hand CDs and old LPs.

2 What does MPB stand for?

Vendedora	Você precisa de ajuda?
David	Oi! Estou à procura de música típica do Brasil. O que você sugere?
Vendedora	Tem estes CDs de bossa nova, de samba, de música sertaneja, e estes são de MPB. Estão todos na oferta, com preços baratíssimos.
David	MPB – o que é isso?
Vendedora	Música Popular Brasileira – todo mundo gosta! A variedade é enorme.
David	E aquele, o que é?
Vendedora	Este grupo é novo, mas o disco é o mais vendido do verão, já venderam mais de 25 mil CDs; é um ritmo típico do nordeste – se chama forró.
David	Então, dê-me esses três por favor. Obrigado pela ajuda.

3 Read the conversations again and answer true or false.

a The most fashionable products at the moment are plastic belts.

b David is shown three different types of CD.

c The best-selling CD of the summer is by a new group.

Language discovery 2

1. **Find the expressions meaning the same as: muito lindas / muito baratos.**
2. **What's the expression for How about ... ? / What about ...?**
3. **How many CDs have the best-selling group sold? How might you say 48 thousand?**
4. **Which two expressions both mean give me?**

1 -ÍSSIMO *VERY ...*

A nice alternative to using **muito** + adjective (*very / really* ...) is to add **-íssimo(a)** to the end of the adjective. For the majority of adjectives (ending in **-o** or **-e**), remove the last letter and add **-íssim(a)** instead (remembering to use the correct ending depending on whether the noun in question is masculine or feminine):

lindo ⟶ lindíssimo: esta ilha é lindíssima

inteligente ⟶ inteligentíssimo: os estudantes são inteligentíssimos

Note that **ótimo** is used to mean **muito bom** and **péssimo** to mean **muito mau**:

Esta revista é péssima!	*This magazine is awful!*

2 RECOMMENDING, SUGGESTING AND REQUESTING ADVICE

O que você sugere / recomenda / acha / aconselha? *What do you suggest / recommend / think / advise?*

Que tal ...?	*What / How about ...?*
Por que não ...?	*Why not ...?*
Por que não compra o azul?	*Why don't you buy the blue one?*

You can reply using **Você tem razão** *You're right*; **(Não) concordo com você** *I (don't) agree with you.*

3 NUMBERS GREATER THAN 1,000 – AN OVERVIEW

The word for *one thousand* (**mil**) never changes its form: **dois mil, quarenta mil, setecentos mil**. Portuguese uses a full stop in written numbers where in English a comma would be used: **1.567** *1,567*; **38.900** *38,900*. Years are expressed as a full number, e.g. 1985 = **mil, novecentos e oitenta e cinco**. You should apply the previous rules for forming the hundreds and tens, including feminine forms. The joining word **e** (*and*) is used after the thousand only when the thousand is followed directly by a number from 1 to 100, e.g. 2,065 = **dois mil e sessenta e cinco**, or when the thousand is followed by a number ending in 00, e.g. 16,800 = **dezesseis mil e oitocentos**.

4 ME DÁ / DÊ-ME *GIVE ME*

The grammatically correct way to say *give me* is **dê-me**; however, what you hear much of the time is the more casual **me dá**. Other examples of a more relaxed approach to the rules include: **me mostra** instead of **mostre-me** (*show me*), **me telefona** instead of **telefone-me** (*call me*), **me manda uma mensagem / um email** instead of **mande-me ...** (*send me a message / an email*), **me conta** instead of **me conte** (*tell me*). Remember that many languages have different formal and informal words and constructions – just be alert to different forms as you listen.

Practice 2

1 **Complete with the correct form of the adjective ending in -íssimo.**

a Estes sapatos estão (muito apertados) (*too tight*) __________.

b Estas camisas são (baratas) _______.

c Uma decisão (muito certa) _______!

d O novo filme é (muito chato) (*awful / boring*) _______.

e Os ingressos são (muito caros) _______.

2 08.07 **Listen and note down in English what is recommended or suggested.**

a ______________________________

b ______________________________

c ______________________________

3 08.08 **Listen and choose the correct number in each case.**

a	2.518	2.508	25.518
b	1974	1965	1975
c	36.004	36.400	36.014
d	1.089	1.088	11.089
e	72.262	62.462	72.462

4 **Convert the underlined verbs in Amélia's message to Mariana from formal to informal forms.**

Oi Mariana! Tudo bem?

Amiga, telefone-me ou (*or*) mande-me um email porque (*because*) quero saber suas notícias (*news*). Conte-me tudo!

Um beijo (*a kiss*)!

Reading

NA LOJA DE DEPARTAMENTOS

1 Try to guess which department of the store you would visit to buy the following items.

1. → Moda	5. → Eletrodomésticos
2. → Perfumaria	6. → Casa (móveis e têxteis)
3. → Esportes	7. → Alimentação
4. → Aparelhos elétricos & eletrônicos	8. → Cultura e Lazer

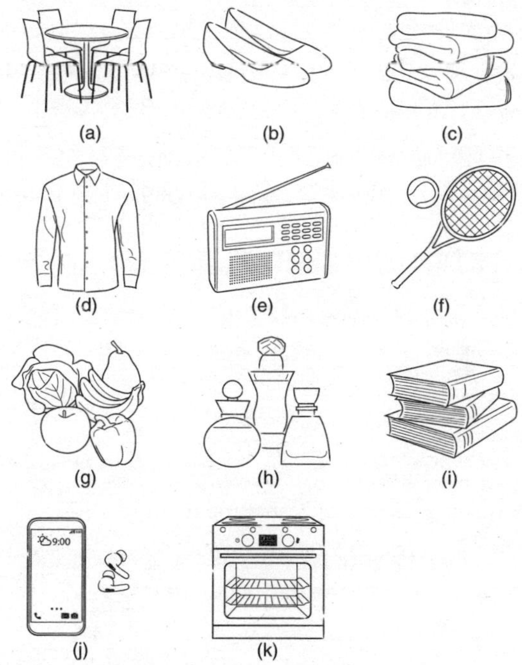

2 08.09 Pronunciation practice

The letter **x** in Portuguese has different sounds, but it's not always easy to decide which way to pronounce it when you first come across new words, as the rules are not rigid. You need to note down the spelling and sound of the words as you discover them. Listen now to two words you heard in the dialogues: the expression for *let me see* (**deixe ver**) and the verb *to try on* (**experimentar**) – the letter **x** is pronounced differently in each one. Listen to the audio and practice some more examples.

Go further

Read the following important phrases and practice saying them out loud.

Na loja	*in the shop.*
Posso ver ...?	*Can I see ...?*
Posso provar / experimentar?	*Can I try it on?*
Prefiro este / esta.	*I prefer this one.*
É muito pequeno(a) / grande(a).	*It's too small / big.*
Tem menor?	*Do you have a smaller size?*
Tem maior?	*Do you have a larger size?*
É muito curto(a) / longo(a).	*It's very short / long.*
Não gosto da cor / do estilo.	*I don't like the color / the style.*
Estou só vendo.	*I'm only looking / browsing.*

Listen and understand

08.10 **Listen to Jorge buying a shirt and answer the questions:**

1 What style of shirt is he looking for?

2 What is his size?

3 Which color does he prefer?

Speaking

Let's practice! Now it's your turn to ask for help in a shop. Fill in the gaps and say your part of the dialogue out loud.

Funcionária	Quer ajuda?
You	Tem ... / Queria ... / Posso ver... *(say what you want)*?
Funcionária	Que tamanho?
You	Pequeno / Médio / Grande / GG or 42, 44, 46, 48, etc.
Funcionária	Que cor prefere?
You	Prefiro *(say which colour you prefer)* ...
Funcionária	Mais alguma coisa?
You	Não, isso é tudo. Obrigado(a).

Test yourself

1 Follow the clues to find the clothing or accessories.

a sandálias brasileiras famosas H _ _ _ _ _ _ _ _

b para saber as horas, precisa de um R _ _ _ _ _ _

c se usam nos pés S _ _ _ _ _ _

d roupa masculina formal T _ _ _ _

e para uma festa *(party)*, um ... elegante V _ _ _ _ _ _

2 08.11 **Listen and decide if each statement is true or false.**

a He's looking for a brown jacket.

b She likes Paulo's green flip-flops.

c He only has hats in red or purple.

d She suggests new bags in yellow or white.

SELF CHECK

	I CAN ...
⚪	. . . ask for clothing and other items by color and size.
⚪	. . . understand and react to recommendations and suggestions.
⚪	. . . specify *this*, *that*, *these* and *those*.
⚪	. . . request information about products.
⚪	. . . understand numbers above 1,000.

9

In this unit, you will learn how to:

» talk about future plans.
» say what you would like to do.
» accept or decline invitations.
» recognize typical Brazilian celebrations.
» discuss typical holiday activities.

Planos para o feriado

My progress tracker

DAY / DATE	Listen	Speak	Read	Write	Converse
	○	○	○	○	○
	○	○	○	○	○
	○	○	○	○	○
	○	○	○	○	○
	○	○	○	○	○

Celebrações

Festas de aniversário de crianças (*children's birthday parties*) can be **eventos grandes** (*large events*), and also **muito caros**. Not only are children invited, but so are **a família toda, os vizinhos** (*the neighbours*) **e os amigos** are also invited. A *special venue* (**um salão de festas**) is sometimes hired to fit everyone in and to keep the kids entertained. **Batizados** (*christenings*) are important family occasions that bring relatives and friends together. When a girl reaches 15, the occasion can be marked with a **Festa de Quinze Anos** (*fifteenth birthday party*). In many families, instead of a party, the occasion can be marked with **um presente especial, uma viagem** or **uma reunião de família**. **Casamentos** (*weddings*) can be big affairs, and most take place in the evening. A reception follows a church ceremony, where finger food and cake are served. Nowadays some couples decide to register their commitment to each other as a **relação estável** (*stable relationship*), which guarantees legal rights. This option is open to both hetero- and homosexual couples.

What have you been invited to if you receive an invitation to a batizado, aniversário, festa de quinze anos or casamento?

Vocabulary builder

09.01 Look at the words and phrases and complete the missing English expressions. Then listen and try to imitate the pronunciation of the speakers.

FÉRIAS, FERIADOS E CELEBRAÇÕES	*HOLIDAYS, BANK HOLIDAYS AND CELEBRATIONS*
as Festas Juninas	*'June' festivals (celebrating Saints Antônio, João and Pedro)*
o Natal	*Christmas*
o Reveillon	*New Year's Eve*
a Páscoa	*Easter*
a Semana Santa	*Holy _______*
o Carnaval	_______
o feriado	*bank holiday*
o Dia da Independência	_______ *Day (7 September)*
o Dia da Proclamação da República	*Day of the Proclamation of the Republic (15 November)*

ATIVIDADES	*ACTIVITIES*
ir ao clube	*to go to a club*
fazer um churrasco	*to have a barbecue*
visitar a família	_______
ir para a praia	*to go to a beach*
viajar	*to travel*
ir pescar	*to go fishing*
ir pro (= para o) interior / litoral	*to go to the country / to the coast*
fazer uma trilha	*to go hiking*

NEW EXPRESSIONS

09.02 Look at the words and expressions that are used in the following conversation. Note their meanings.

Tô (= Estou) pensando em visitar	*I'm thinking about visiting.*
Estávamos pensando	*We were thinking.*
Você quer ir conosco?	*Do you want to go with us?*

seria ótimo, mas não tem jeito	*it would be great, but it won't work / won't be possible*
o feriado inteirinho	*the whole bank holiday*
na fazenda	*on the farm / family estate*
sobrinho	*nephew*
pipoca	*popcorn*
amendoim torrado	*roasted peanut(s)*
um montão de coisas	*a pile of things*
fim de semana	*weekend*

Conversation 1

09.03 *Colleagues Sebastião and Irene are discussing their plans for the bank holiday.*

1 How were Sebastião and his family planning on spending the bank holiday?

Sebastião	Então, Irene, você tem planos para o feriado?
Irene	Tô pensando em visitar minha família no interior. E você, Sebastião?
Sebastião	Não sei exatamente. Estávamos pensando em passar umas horinhas no clube. Meus filhos adoram ficar na piscina.
Irene	Quem não gosta?
Sebastião	Você quer ir conosco?
Irene	Ah, Sebastião, seria ótimo, mas não tem jeito. Vou passar o feriado inteirinho na fazenda; tem o batizado do meu sobrinho.
Sebastião	Ah é? Vocês vão fazer churrasco?
Irene	Vamos sim, e as crianças querem pipoca, amendoim torrado, um montão de coisas, sabe?
Sebastião	Tá. Então por que não vem com a gente no próximo fim de semana?
Irene	Tudo bem, Sebastião. Obrigadíssima pelo convite!

2 Read the conversation again, and with the help of the new expressions, answer the questions.

a What do Sebastião's children love doing?

b What event is Irene's family celebrating?

c When does Sebastião suggest that Irene goes with them to the club?

3 **Now listen to the dialogue again, pausing the audio and repeating after each line.**

Language discovery 1

1 **Which expressions mean** *I am thinking* **and** *We were thinking*? **Which two Portuguese verbs are used in each case?**

2 **Find two different ways of expressing** *with us*; **which is formal and which is informal?**

3 **The word montão comes from the word for** *hill* **(monte); what effect does the -ão ending give it?**

4 **Find the singular form of these words: fins de semana, amendoins.**

1 I AM / I WAS THINKING OF DOING

An action going on at the moment is expressed by taking the present tense of **estar** + the verb in its **-ando / -endo / -indo** format. **Pensar** + **em** + the verb in the infinitive means *to think of / about ...ing*:

Estamos pensando em comprar uma casa. *We're thinking of buying a house.*

To express the same idea in the past (*was / were thinking of* ...), use **estar** in the following forms:

eu estava	**nós estávamos**
ele / ela / você estava	**eles / elas / vocês estavam**
Eles estavam pensando em passar o carnaval em Fortaleza.	*They were thinking of spending carnival in Fortaleza.*

2 PRONOUNS WITH COM

Com a gente is the colloquial way to say *with us*; the more standard way is **conosco**; similarly **comigo** means *with me*. For all other *with* expressions (*with him*, *with her*, etc.), use **com** + subject pronouns: **com ele**, **com ela**, **com você**, **com eles**, and so on. You will also hear **contigo**, meaning *with you*, often in song lyrics.

Eu vou com vocês.	*I'm going / I go with you.*
Ela não quer ir com eles.	*She doesn't want to go with them.*

3 UM MONTÃO – THE ENDING -ÃO

By using **-ão** to alter the end of words, you can create the effect of something appearing *larger*, *grander*, *stronger*, *uglier*, etc. Typical examples include:

carta *letter* ⟶ **cartão** *card*

porta *door* ⟶ **portão** *gate*

sala *room* ⟶ **salão** *hall / ballroom*

Usually the original feminine gender of a word changes to masculine.

4 IRREGULAR PLURALS: M ⟶ NS

Nouns and adjectives ending in **-m** form their plural by changing the **-m** to **-ns**:

homem *man* ⟶ **homens** *men*

viagem ⟶ **viagens**

comum *common* ⟶ **comuns**

Practice 1

1 **Match the Portuguese to the English.**

- **a** Estou pensando em arranjar outro emprego.
- **b** Estavam pensando em vender o carro.
- **c** Ela estava pensando em fazer um curso de Aviação.
- **d** Você está pensando em sair no sábado?
- **e** O que você estava pensando em fazer?

- **1** She was thinking of doing a flying course.
- **2** What were you thinking of doing?
- **3** I'm thinking of looking for another job.
- **4** They were thinking about selling the car.
- **5** Are you thinking of going out on Saturday?

2 09.04 **Listen and select which one you hear.**

- **a** Mônica quer sair com eles / com você.
- **b** João, você vem conosco / comigo?
- **c** Eles não podem ir com a gente / com ela.
- **d** Posso ir com ele / contigo?

3 Replace the words in italics with a word or expression from the box. Write out your answers.

gatão	cachorrão	um tempão
beijão	abração	um garrafão

a Paula tem um *gato enorme*.
b Estamos esperando o ônibus por *muito tempo*.
c Temos sede; precisamos comprar *uma garrafa gigante* de água.
d A Joana tem um *cachorro enorme* chamado Tufão.
e Um *beijo grande* pra (= para a) tia Cecília.
f Um *abraço grande* pra você.

4 Add the missing singular or plural forms.

Singular	Plural
jardim	
mensagem	
	sons (*sounds*)
bombom (*sweet*)	
	nuvens (*clouds*)

Conversation 2

NEW EXPRESSIONS

09.05 **Look at the words and expressions that are used in the following conversation. Note their meanings.**

Que sorte!	*What luck! / How lucky!*
Faz um tempão que não vou para a praia.	*It's ages since I went to the beach.*
Que saudade!	*How I miss it!*
vale a pena	*it's worth it*
gostaria	*I would like.*
Não acredito!	*I don't believe it!*
Vai ser o máximo!	*It's going to be brilliant!*
e tal	*and so on / and stuff*
tão legal	*so great*
Mal posso esperar!	*I can hardly wait!*

09.06 *Arnaldo and Beatriz are chatting about their holiday plans.*

1 How long is Arnaldo going to spend at the beach?

Beatriz	Arnaldo, o que você vai fazer durante as férias?
Arnaldo	Eu vou passar oito dias no litoral com meus primos.
Beatriz	Que sorte! Faz um tempão que não vou para a praia. Ai, que saudade!
Arnaldo	Então, vem comigo, Beatriz! Sempre vale a pena – praia, sol, cerveja ...
Beatriz	Ah, Arnaldo, você sabe que eu gostaria muito de ir com você, mas não posso.
Arnaldo	Cê vai pra onde?
Beatriz	Vou viajar com a Cecília – vamos para Nova Iorque.
Arnaldo	Não acredito! Vai ser o máximo! Eu também gostaria de ir lá contigo, fazer compras e tal.
Beatriz	Vai ser tão legal, mal posso esperar!

2 Read the conversation again and answer the following questions:

a How does Arnaldo try to tempt Beatriz to go to the beach with him?

b What is Beatriz going to be doing?

c How is Beatriz feeling about the trip?

LANGUAGE TIP

Use any of the following when making arrangements to meet:

tem jeito para quarta-feira	*Wednesday will work / Wednesday is do-able*
não tem jeito para quarta-feira	*Wednesday won't work / Wednesday isn't do-able*
vai dar certo	*that will work*
não vai dar certo	*that isn't going to work*
acho que dá para sexta-feira	*I think Friday will work / I think Friday is do-able*
acho que não dá para sexta-feira	*I don't think Friday will work / I don't think Friday is do-able*

These are all colloquial expressions; you could instead use the less informal **é / não é possível** *that is / isn't possible*.

LANGUAGE TIP

Colloquial expressions:

cê = você	
pro / pra = para o / para a	
super-...	*really...*
beleza!	*fantastic!*
saudade	*nostalgia / homesickness / missing a person or place*

Language discovery 2

1 **How does Beatriz express how long it is since she went to the beach?**
2 **How do you say to someone** *come with me***?**
3 **Which is the verb form meaning** *I would like ...***?**
4 **If tão legal means** *so great***, what might tão bom mean? How would you say** *so cheap***?**

1 FAZ ... QUE (NÃO) ... *IT'S ... SINCE I ...*

Faz + time reference + **que** + present tense = *it's ... since I / we / he, etc. did ...*:

Faz uma hora que eu estou esperando na fila. *I have been waiting for an hour in the queue.*

Faz um tempão que nós não vamos ao cinema. *It's a long time since we went to the cinema.*

Faz dez anos que eu não viajo para outro país. *It's been ten years since I traveled to another country.*

2 COMMANDS AS INVITATIONS: *COME / GO WITH ME*

Remember that many Brazilians use the more casual forms of verb commands, but you may hear both formal and informal versions. Listen out for the following:

Formal version	Informal version	
venha	**vem**	*come*
vá	**vai**	*go*
olhe	**olha**	*look*
escute	**escuta**	*listen*
ouça	**ouve**	*hear / listen*
tome	**toma**	*take*
diga	**diz**	*say / tell*
pergunte	**pergunta**	*ask*
responda	**responde**	*answer*

3 EXPRESSING *WOULD LIKE (TO) ...*

gostaria ... *I / he / she / you* (sing) *would like (to) ...*

gostaríamos ... *we would like (to) ...*

gostariam ... *they / you* (pl) *would like (to) ...*

Don't forget to follow the verb with **de** before another verb:

Eu gostaria de viajar.	*I would like to travel.*
O que você gostaria de fazer esta noite?	*What would you like to do tonight?*
Não gostaríamos de visitar a selva.	*We wouldn't like to visit the jungle.*

4 TÃO / TANTO *SO / SO MUCH*

Tão is used before adjectives:

Este vinho é tão caro.	*This wine is so expensive.*
As senhoras são tão simpáticas.	*The women are so kind.*

Use **tanto (a / os / as)** with nouns:

Tanta poluição neste rio!	*So much pollution in this river!*
Há tantas pessoas que não consigo ver nada.	*There are so many people that I can't see anything.*

Tanto is also used after verbs:

Ela precisa tanto sair de férias.	*She really needs to go on holiday.*

Practice 2

1 09.07 **Listen to Fátima saying how long it is since she did various things, and decide if the statements are true or false.**
- **a** It's three years since she visited Salvador.
- **b** It's ages since she spoke with her cousin.
- **c** It's two weeks since she went to the club.
- **d** It's a month since she went to the beach.

2 **Translate into English.**
- **a** Artur, vem conosco!
- **b** Tome o seu troco (*change*)!
- **c** Venha conhecer o novo shopping!
- **d** Carla, escuta minha mensagem e me responde!

3 **Match the questions and answers.**

a Quer acampar no fim de semana?	**1** Gostariam de relaxar.
b Vocês gostariam de sair amanhã?	**2** Ela vai fazer uma entrevista de emprego.

c O que Cíntia vai fazer hoje?
d Como eles gostariam de passar o feriado?

3 Não. Detesto acampar!
4 Sim, gostaríamos de jantar fora.

4 Complete the sentences with tão or the correct form of tanto.

a Esta empresa paga ______ pouco!
b Elas falam _______ sem parar!
c Tem _______ bolos que não sei qual escolher (*to choose*).
d Hoje está _______ frio que não vamos para a praia.

Reading

Look at Rute's diary for the next week of her holidays and answer the following questions in Portuguese.

segunda-feira	Festa junina no Parque da Cidade às 7 da noite
terça-feira	Campeonato de vôlei de praia (o dia todo)
quarta-feira	Dia livre
quinta-feira	Jantar com meus pais
sexta-feira	Festa de aniversário do Carlos
sábado	Praia de manhã e casamento da Ana à noite

1 Onde a Rute vai na segunda-feira de noite?
2 Quem ela vai encontrar na quinta-feira?
3 Quando é a festa de aniversário do Carlos?
4 Quando ela vai à praia?
5 O que ela vai fazer na terça-feira?

Listen and understand

09.08 **Listen to a message left on Ricardo's voicemail by a friend and answer the following questions.**

1 What is he being invited to?
2 Who can he take with him?
3 When is this event going to be?

Writing

Now reply to Jorge's invitation by email, as though you were Ricardo. Follow the cues and create your response.

1 **Greet Jorge.**
2 **Thank him for the invitation.**
3 **Say** *It would be great but it's not possible; we're going to spend Sunday at the beach.*
4 **Say** *Happy birthday* **(Parabéns!).**
5 **Sign off.**

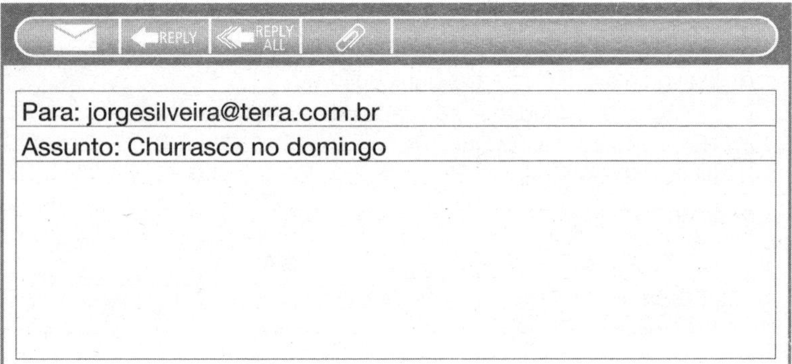

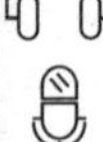

09.09 **Pronunciation practice**

The letter **g** has different sounds according to what vowel follows it. Listen now to some examples from the dialogues, plus some additional words, giving you a better idea of pronunciation rules.

Go further

9.10 **The birthday song in Portuguese sounds exactly like it does in English, but the words are a bit different. Can you guess what each line means?**

Parabéns pra você
Nesta data querida
Muitas felicidades
Muitos anos de vida!

Test yourself

1 Identify the odd one out in each of the following.

a Natal – Reveillon – Páscoa – domingo
b visitar família – viajar – trabalhar – ir ao clube
c não tem jeito – dá certo – não posso – não dá
d irmão – montão – tempão – portão

2 Match the colloquial expressions.

a Tantos perrengues!	**1** How I miss that!
b Beleza!	**2** So many difficulties!
c Que saudade!	**3** Is that so?
d Que legal!	**4** How brilliant!
e Ah é?	**5** Fantastic!

3 Try saying the following sentences out loud in Portuguese.

a Do you have plans for the bank holiday?
b I'm going to spend the weekend on the coast.
c Thanks for the invitation!
d I'd like to visit Brasília.
e I can hardly wait!

SELF CHECK

I CAN ...
... talk about future plans.
... say what I would like to do.
... accept or decline invitations.
... recognize typical Brazilian celebrations.
... discuss typical holiday activities.

10

In this unit, you will learn how to:

» talk about past events.
» discuss sports and leisure activities.
» ask and answer questions in the past.
» describe how good or bad something was.
» recognize time references in the past.

Você viu o jogo?

My progress tracker

DAY / DATE	Listening	Speaking	Reading	Writing	Conversation
	○	○	○	○	○
	○	○	○	○	○
	○	○	○	○	○
	○	○	○	○	○
	○	○	○	○	○

Lazer

The warm climate makes it possible to spend a lot of leisure time outdoors – **na praia**, **no parque**, **no jardim**, near **cachoeiras** (*waterfalls*) or along **lagos** (*lakes*) or **rios** (*rivers*). Brazilians of all ages love **parques de diversão** (*amusement parks*), and these can get extremely busy in the **alta temporada** (*high season*)! **Futebol** is played on any surface (sand, cement, grass). Volleyball (indoor and outdoor) is also very popular. Many Brazilians have never seen **geada** (*frost*) or **neve** (*snow*), so there are few opportunities for cold-weather activities outdoors – in fact, many people cancel their day out if it starts to rain! Many spend a lot of time on their computers and mobile phones, on social media, checking the news and the weather, and so on. In social gatherings, Brazilians like to talk about **política** (*politics*), particularly at local level, and **a economia** (*the economy*). Discussions can become very heated and animated, with everybody speaking loudly and at the same time. Restaurants and bars can be very noisy places, as can the family dinner table! Of course, **o jogo** (*the game / match*) is another well-contested debate, whichever team you support.

If you want to save money, when is the best time to go to this amusement park?

Parque Beto Carrero World

Entrada Adultos: 1 dia R$80 2 dias R$130

Crianças de 4 a 9 anos: 1 dia R$60 2 dias R$100

Crianças a partir de 10 anos pagam como adultos.

Os preços acima são válidos apenas na baixa temporada!

Vocabulary builder

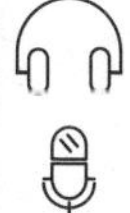

10.01 **Look at the words and phrases and complete the missing English expressions. Then listen and try to imitate the pronunciation of the speakers.**

ESPORTES E LAZER	*SPORTS AND LEISURE*
jogar vôlei / basquete	*to play volleyball / basketball*
fazer caminhadas no calçadão	*to stroll along the promenade*
correr na praia	*to run on the beach*
relaxar	________
ir à academia	*to go to the gym*
encontrar / sair com amigos	*to meet / go out with friends*
ir a uma boate / um show de música	*to go to a club / a music show*
dançar	________
ir ao cinema / teatro	*to go to the cinema /* ________
ir ao shopping	*to go to the shopping centre*
ver Fórmula 1	*to watch* (lit. *to see*) *Formula 1*
assistir TV / uma novela	*to watch TV / a soap opera*

QUESTIONS IN THE PAST TENSE	
O que você fez / viu / comeu?	*What did you do / see / eat?*
Onde você foi / visitou?	*Where did you go /* ________*?*
O que você achou?	*What did you think?*
Você gostou?	*Did you enjoy / like it?*
O que aconteceu?	*What happened?*
Como foi?	*What was it like / How was it?*

NEW EXPRESSIONS

10.02 Look at the words and expressions that are used in the following conversation. Note their meanings.

Você viu o jogo ontem à noite?	*Did you see the match last night?*
Não pude assistir.	*I couldn't watch (it).*
Que pena!	*What a shame!*
eles começaram mal	*they started badly*
E daí?	*And then what?*
Daí, virou uma porcaria!	*And then it turned into a shambles!*
o capitão brigou com o árbitro	*the captain argued with the referee*
o Santos ganhou	*Santos won.*
Deus me livre de futebol!	*God forbid, football!* (lit. *God free me from football!*)
Eu fui ao cinema.	*I went to the cinema.*

Conversation 1

10.03 *Gabriel and Iolanda are in a bar chatting about last night's football.*

1 How does Gabriel describe the match?

Gabriel	Iolanda, você viu o jogo ontem à noite?
Iolanda	Não vi, não. Eu estava trabalhando até tarde e não pude assistir.
Gabriel	Que pena! Foi ótimo!
Iolanda	O que aconteceu, então?
Gabriel	O Botafogo estava ganhando, mas na segunda parte eles começaram mal.
Iolanda	E daí?
Gabriel	Daí, virou uma porcaria! O capitão brigou com o árbitro e recebeu o cartão vermelho.
Iolanda	Incrível! E depois?
Gabriel	Bom, no fim, o Santos ganhou e todo o mundo gostou. Maravilha!
(Another friend, Mário, approaches).	
Iolanda	Mário, tudo bem? Estávamos falando do jogo. Você viu?
Mário	Eu, não! Deus me livre de futebol! Detesto! Eu fui ao cinema; o filme foi interessantíssimo.

2 Read the conversation again and match the questions and answers.

a Você viu o jogo?
b O que aconteceu?
c E daí?
d E depois?

1 O Botafogo estava ganhando.
2 No fim, o Santos ganhou.
3 Não vi, não.
4 Daí, virou uma porcaria.

HOW TO EXPRESS PAST SEQUENCES

primeiro	*first*
depois	*then, after*
daí	*and then*
assim	*then, therefore*
então	*and so*
no fim	*in the end*

gosto (muito) / não gosto (nada)	*I like (a lot) / I don't like (at all)*
adoro / detesto	*I love / hate*
não me interessa	*it doesn't interest me*

Language discovery 1

1 **Find the Portuguese for the following expressions in the dialogue:** *everybody enjoyed / had a good time*; *he received the red card*; *they started badly*.

2 **Work out the meaning of the following verbs, all in the first person singular (*I*): não vi; não pude; eu fui.**

3 **Which adjectives describe the football match and the film? Which verb is used with both, meaning** *it was***?**

1 EXPRESSING THE SIMPLE PAST: *I WENT, I ATE, I ENJOYED*

To express what you did, or what you have done, at a specific point in the past, remove the **-ar**, **-er**, **-ir** ending from the infinitive form of a regular verb and follow the pattern for past tense endings as follows:

	-ar → gostar	-er → beber	-ir → abrir
eu	**+ei → gostei**	**+i → bebi**	**+i → abri**
você / ele / ela	**+ou → gostou**	**+eu → bebeu**	**+iu → abriu**
nós	**+amos → gostamos**	**+emos → bebemos**	**+imos → abrimos**
vocês / eles / elas	**+aram → gostaram**	**+eram → beberam**	**+iram → abriram**

Look for patterns to help you remember, e.g. **amos / emos / imos**. These are also the endings used for the *we* verb form in the present tense – you need to look out for past time references to help you distinguish between the two timeframes. This past tense is often called the preterite.

2 IRREGULAR VERBS IN THE PRETERITE: VER / PODER / IR

ver: vi, viu, vimos, viram

poder: pude, pôde, pudemos, puderam

ir: fui, foi, fomos, foram

You will use the preterite of **ir** a lot to express where you went in the past.

3 DESCRIBING HOW SOMETHING WAS: FOI + ADJECTIVE

The Portuguese verb **ser** has the same form in the preterite as **ir**: **fui**, **foi**, **fomos**, **foram**. In practice, it is used extensively in the **foi** form to express *it was* when describing what something was like: **foi ótimo / maravilhoso / interessante / péssimo / ruim** (*awful*) **/ horrível / divertido** (*funny*), etc. Don't forget to change the ending of the adjective if you are describing something feminine.

Practice 1

1 Form the verbs correctly in the past tense.

a Eu (relaxar) ________ no clube.
b Ingrid (perder = *to lose*) ________ a carteira (*purse / wallet*).
c Vocês (assistir) ________ o programa sobre a Amazonia?
d Nós não (visitar) ________ o Jardim Botânico.
e O ladrão *(thief)* (desaparecer = *to disappear*) ________.

2 Choose the correct response.

a Vocês viram o futebol ontem?
1 Sim, vimos. **2** Sim, vi.

b A Tainá jogou tênis com você?
1 Não, ela não pude. **2** Não, ela não pôde.

c Onde você foi no sábado?
1 Foi à academia. **2** Fui à academia.

3 10.04 **Listen and choose how each event is described.**

a The film was great / terrible.
b The show was marvellous / boring.
c The game was awful / incredible.
d The soap opera was interesting / funny.

Conversation 2

NEW EXPRESSIONS

10.05 Look at the words and expressions that are used in the following conversation. Note their meanings.

Decidi ir ao shopping.	*I decided to go to the shopping centre.*
Aproveitei as ofertas	*I took advantage of the offers/discounts.*
já que ...	*(seeing) as ... / given that*
Tive que voltar antes do fim.	*I had to go home* (lit. *return*) *before the end.*
Não fiz nada.	*I didn't do anything.*
Fiquei em casa.	*I stayed at home.*

10.06 *Priscila and Vicente are chatting on the phone about what they did at the weekend.*

1 What did Priscila buy?

Vicente	Oi, Priscila, tudo bem? Me conta, o que você fez no fim de semana?
Priscila	No sábado meus pais estavam visitando a família, então decidi ir ao shopping.
Vicente	O que você comprou?
Priscila	Aproveitei as ofertas e comprei uma bolsa e duas saias. Estavam muito baratas!
Vicente	Bom, já que gosto tanto de música clássica, fui a um show ao vivo na praça.
Priscila	Legal! Foi bom?
Vicente	Foi excelente! A praça estava lotada, mas tive que voltar antes do fim para pegar o ônibus. Foi uma pena!
Priscila	Eu, no domingo, não fiz nada. Fiquei em casa, dormi muito e vi uns filmes na Netflix. E você?
Vicente	Passei o domingo me preparando para uma entrevista na terça-feira.
Priscila	Ah é? Entrevista pra quê? Qual é o emprego?
Vicente	É para gerente de mídia social.

2 **Read, then listen to, the whole conversation again and answer the questions.**

a What were Priscila's parents doing on Saturday?

b Where did Vicente go?

c Why did he have to leave early?

d What did Priscila do on Sunday?

> **LANGUAGE TIP**
>
> Remember! Casual language: **me diverti / me encontrei / me conta**; formal language: **diverti-me / encontrei-me / conte-me**

Language discovery 2

1 **Find the expressions in the dialogue that mean:** *I didn't do anything / I had to return / social media manager*.

2 **Which -ar verb does fiquei come from?**

3 **Which preposition, denoting** *in / on / at*, **comes before ...?**

____ fim de semana; ____ sábado;
____ domingo; _____ terça-feira.

1 MORE IRREGULAR PRETERITES: FAZER (*TO DO, MAKE*) / TER (*TO HAVE*) / DIZER (*TO SAY, TELL*)

Fazer: fiz / fez / fizemos / fizeram

Ter: tive / teve / tivemos / tiveram

Dizer: disse / disse / dissemos / disseram

2 SPELLING CHANGES IN THE PRETERITE: VERBS ENDING IN -CAR AND -GAR

In the first person (*I*) in the preterite, compare what happens with a regular **-ar** verb and those ending in **-car** and **-gar**:

comprar ⟶ **comprei**

ficar ⟶ **fiquei**

pagar ⟶ **paguei**

-car and **-gar** verbs do this to maintain a hard **c** or **g** sound. Without the change, the letters **c** and **g** when followed by **e** make soft sounds, and would therefore deviate from the sound of the original verb. More typical examples include: **brincar** *to play*, **explicar** *to explain*, **tocar** *to touch / to play an instrument*, **chegar** *to arrive*, **jogar** *to play sport / games*, **entregar** *to hand over*.

3 EXPRESSING THE PAST: *LAST WEEK*, *ON MONDAY*, ETC.

Use time references you already know along with a verb in the preterite to denote an event that has already happened, e.g.,

no sábado fomos ao clube	*on Saturday we went to the leisure center*
na quarta-feira trabalhei	*on Wednesday I worked*

Other useful time expressions include: **no domingo passado, a semana passada**, **o ano passado**, etc.; **ontem** (*yesterday*); **ontem à noite**, **ontem de manhã**, **ontem de tarde**. Don't forget you can also use references to clock time, such as **às dez e vinte ela pegou o ônibus**.

Practice 2

1 Choose the correct verb form.

- **a** Eu fiz / fez uma bagunça dentro do armário (*a mess inside the cupboard*).
- **b** Vocês tiveram / tivemos muita sorte.
- **c** O que ela disseram / disse?
- **d** Nós não fez / fizemos barulho (*noise*).
- **e** Marcos teve / tive que ir trabalhar no sábado.

2 Form the verbs correctly in the preterite.

- **a** jogar ⟶ Eu ________ vôlei na praia.
- **b** explicar ⟶ O professor ________ a lição.
- **c** brincar ⟶ Eu não ________ ontem.
- **d** pagar ⟶ Você ________ a conta?
- **e** chegar ⟶ Eu ________ às 11 horas.

3 Translate into Portuguese. Say the sentences out loud.

- **a** Last week I played basketball.
- **b** Yesterday we went to the theatre.
- **c** The film ended at 9.30 p.m.
- **d** On Thursday she went to the gym.

Reading and writing

1 You go to the beach and see this sign. Can you get the gist of it and say whether each statement is true or false? You may have to do this for real on a beach in Brazil!

a This is an advert for a surfing competition.
b It is dangerous to swim in the sea today.
c It is a good day for sailing.
d You are advised to stay away from the sea today.

2 Gabriela is on holiday in Florianópolis with her family. After a fun day at Beto Carrero World, one of the largest amusement parks in Brazil, she sends an email to her friends in Brasília. Fill in the gaps in the text with the correct word.

dentro dormir no cara tanto

REPLY REPLY ALL

Oi gente! A entrada ______ parque foi ______, mas valeu a pena! Adorei a montanha russa, o barco Viking e os shows ao vivo. Gritamos muito ______ do trem fantasma!!! Adorei! Me diverti ______ que estou pregada! Agora vou ______. Beijinhos, Gabi

montanha russa	*rollercoaster*
fantasma	*ghost*
pregada(o)	(slang) *exhausted, very tired*

3 10.07 **Pronunciation practice**

In Brazilian Portuguese, an **-i** at the end of a word has a different sound from its English equivalent – it's almost as if there were a **w** before it. Listen to some examples now and repeat after the speaker.

Now listen and practice how these common combined vowels sound:

-oi

-ai

-ei

Listen and understand

10.08 **Three people report various incidents to the police. Listen to each one and write down in English what happened in each case.**

	What happened?	When?
João		
Carolina		
Jair		

Go further

Erik and Vilma have just moved home and have sent the following message to all their friends:

Queridos amigos,

Resolvemos mudar para o litoral. Já vendemos nossa casa no interior e compramos um apartamento de dois quartos com varanda no litoral. Agora podemos ir à praia a pé! Que maravilha! Realizamos um sonho antigo!

Abraços a todos,
Erik e Vilma

Now fill in the gaps with the verbs from the text above in the 3rd person plural (eles), in the past tense:

Erik e Vilma ________ mudar para o litoral. Eles já ________ a sua casa no interior e ________ um apartamento no litoral. Agora eles podem ir à praia a pé. Eles ________ um sonho antigo.

Test yourself

1 10.09 **Listen to Fernanda describe her weekend and put the activities in the correct order.**

- **a** ir ao cinema
- **b** passar a manhã no clube
- **c** encontrar Ana
- **d** assistir um show
- **e** ficar em casa
- **f** ir fazer compras
- **g** ver TV

2 Fill the gaps in this dialogue with expressions from the box.

voltei	ontem	ótimo	Adorei!	uma boate

Antônio	Você saiu ________ à noite?
Yuri	Saí, sim. Fui a ________ com meus colegas.
Antônio	Vocês se divertiram?
Yuri	Muitíssimo! Dançamos muito e só ________ para casa às três horas da manhã.
Antônio	Você gostou então?
Yuri	________ Foi ________.

3 Have a go at answering these in Portuguese any way you wish.

- **a** O que você fez ontem?
- **b** Onde você foi no sábado?
- **c** Você gostou da música?
- **d** Como foi o jogo?
- **e** Onde você visitou?

SELF CHECK

	I CAN ...
○	. . . talk about past events.
○	. . . discuss sports and leisure activities.
○	. . . ask and answer questions in the past.
○	. . . describe how good or bad something was.
○	. . . recognize time references in the past.

Review 3

1 **Make full sentences by matching the first part in the left-hand column with the second part from the right-hand column.**

a	Estou pensando em visitar	**1**	na escola.
b	Davide está trabalhando	**2**	pelo interior.
c	Nós estávamos viajando	**3**	chopes.
d	Isabel estava pensando em comprar	**4**	os meus avós.
e	Eles estão bebendo	**5**	uma saia nova.

2 10.10 **Using the cues, follow the dialogue on the audio and say your part during the pauses. You will hear the correct version after each pause.**

a Start by saying *Good afternoon!*
b Say *I have a reservation: a single room reserved for three nights.*
c Give your own name in full.
d Spell your own surname.
e Say *Here.*
f Ask *At what time is breakfast served?*
g Say *Thank you.*

3 10.11 **Listen, and indicate in English what each problem is.**

a ________
b ________
c ________
d ________
e ________

4 **Choose the odd one out in each sequence.**

a	no canto	no fim	ao lado	ao meio-dia
b	hóspede	cama	cofre	despertador
c	calça	terno	preço	vestido
d	amarelo	tamanho	roxo	cinza
e	pescar	jogar	correr	comer

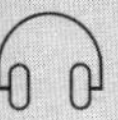

5 10.12 **Listen to people talking about things they have done in the past, and complete the missing information in Portuguese. Use the third person singular or plural (*he / she, they*) of each verb.**

	Quando?	O quê?	Com quem?
a	no fim de semana		
b		teve o batizado da sobrinha	
c			os primos
d	no feriado		
e			as amigas foram / ela não

6 10.13 **Try saying these words out loud, then listen to the correct version on the audio.**

Nova Iorque caixa gente
oi! ritmo bege legal maio
táxi segundo Brasil falei

7 You are looking for clothing in a fashion store. Complete your side of the dialogue.

Funcionária Pois não?
You Say *I would like this Brazil shirt in a large, please.*
Funcionária Prefere com manga curta ou com manga comprida?
You Say *I prefer short sleeves. How much is it?*
Funcionária 140 reais.
You Say *I also want a sun hat.*
Funcionária Estes aqui estão na oferta por 50 reais.
You Say *I will take one. Can I try the shirt on?*
Funcionária À vontade. O provador é no canto, à direita.
(Five minutes later)
You Say *It's very large. Don't you have a smaller one?*
Funcionária Infelizmente não. Só temos G e GG. Na próxima semana ...
You Say *What a shame! Thanks.*

8 10.14 **Listen to a radio advertisement and answer true or false for each question.**

- **a** It's an ad for a new supermarket. T/F
- **b** It's summertime. T/F
- **c** The event is on 16 June. T/F
- **d** The event takes place in Republic Square. T/F
- **e** Listeners are asked to name the most popular film of the summer. T/F
- **f** One of the prizes is a trip to Rio. T/F

9 **Look at the brochure and then complete each sentence with an appropriate word.**

Hotel Fazenda das Amoreiras – a natureza nas suas mãos!

apartamentos de luxo
piscina tropical
quadra de tênis
sala de fitness
passeios a cavalo
atividades para as crianças
5 km de trilhas
lagos
cachoeiras
churrasqueira
bar e música
restaurante

Abertura do restaurante:

Café da manhã: 06:30 – 07:30 – café, sucos e pães de queijo

07:30 – 10:30 – café da manhã buffet

Almoço: 12:30 – 15:00 – almoços e refeições ligeiras

Jantar: A partir das 19:00

O bar 'Flor da Selva' fica aberto das 11:30 até às 02:00 para refeições ligeiras, pizzas, chá e bolos, e uma variedade de bebidas nacionais e internacionais.

No Hotel Fazenda das Amoreiras há várias atividades de lazer nas quais você poderia participar: Pode nadar na ________; pode ________ tênis; pode ________ trilha. Também, você poderia ________ no lago, ________ churrasco, ou dançar no ________.

10 Now answer the following questions.

a What type of accommodation is offered?
b What natural features are advertised?
c What is offered for breakfast for early risers?
d Where can you eat between 3 p.m. and 7 p.m.?
e What is on offer at the 'Flor da Selva' bar as well as pizzas?

Answer key

UNIT 1

Brazil

south region, north region, centre-west region

Vocabulary builder

Greetings Good, How, See you

Conversation 1

1 Ana **2a** morning **b** lawyer **c** José dos Santos **3a** True **b** False **c** False

Language discovery 1

1a Eu **b** Ele **2a** estou **b** sou **3a** está means 'you are/are you' **b** Estou means ' I am'

Practice 1

1a você **b** ele **c** eu **d** nós **2a** médica **b** teacher **c** gerente **d** enfermeira **e** dentista **3a** está **b** Sou **c** Estou **d** é **4a** 3 **b** 4 **c** 1 **d** 2 **5a** Ana – argentina, advogada **b** Peter – alemão, engenheiro **c** Isabel – portuguesa, cozinheira **d** Paulo – brasileiro, médico **6a** nome **b** de / trabalho **c** Sou / própria **d** chamo-me **e** é **7a** Carlos is in a hurry. **b** Joaquim is hungry. **c** Anita is cold. **d** Catarina is hot.

Conversation 2

1 English and Spanish **2a** Italian **b** Toulouse **c** English and German **d** No **e** Ornella's **f** Argentina

Language discovery 2

1a Você fala inglês? **b** falo inglês **2** I am English ... I speak French.

Practice 2

1a -o **b** -am **c** -a **d** -amos **2a** Você não é de Londres. **b** Meu nome não é Kofi. **c** Paulo não fala alemão. **d** Ela não é coreana. **3a** italiana **b** alemão **c** francês **d** espanhola **4a** Falo um pouco de português. **b** Não falo japonês. **c** Falamos francês bem.

Reading
a False **b** False **c** True **d** False

Reading and writing
a agora / em **b** de / mas **c** Sou / moro **d** Sou de Brasília, mas agora moro em Londres **e** (sample answer) Sou de Sydney, mas agora moro em Washington.

Speaking
(sample answers) **1a** Sim, sou australiana. **b** Não, não falo inglês. **c** Sim, o Roberto é de São Paulo. **d** Eu moro em Manchester. **e** Não, ela não tem.

Test yourself
1a 4 **b** 1 **c** 5 **d** 2 **e** 3 **2a** dia / Como **b** Este **c** tudo **d** Muito **e** sou **f** é **3a** Os novos engenheiros são coreanos. **b** Elas não falam português. **c** Eles estão com fome.

UNIT 2

Os brasileiros
João is saying: I'm single, I'm a civil servant and I don't speak English.

Vocabulary builder
Family girlfriend, daughter, sister

Conversation 1
1 Luciana **2a** yes, one son **b** Felipe, Fernando's son **c** Rosa's husband

Language discovery 1
1 tenho **2** vende **3** um, uma – masculine and feminine

Practice 1
1a tem **b** tenho **c** temos **d** tem **e** têm **f** tem **2a** vende **b** como **c** bebem **d** escrevemos **e** corre **3a** meu irmão **b** a foto **c** o funcionário público **d** a mãe **4a** 125 **b** 54 **c** 77 **d** 510 **5a** Fábio is 21. **b** He studies civil engineering. **c** Heloísa is 19. **d** Their mother is a nurse.

Conversation 2
1 22 years old **2a** True **b** True **c** False **d** False **e** True

Language discovery 2

1 bonita **2** mais velho **3** seis meses **4** singular and plural

Practice 2

1a 2 **b** 4 **c** 1 **d** 3 **2a** 3 **b** 2 **c** 1 **d** 4 **3a** Faço anos em março. **b** Ele fazer aniversário em dezembro. **c** Quando você fazer aniversário? **d** Eles fazem um café muito bom. **4a** as minhas irmãs **b** os seus empregados **c** as nossas casas **d** os meus tios

Reading and writing

1 é / em / de / Tenho / sou / minha / dois / no **2a** She is 25. **b** She was born in Taubaté. **c** She is single. **d** She lives in São Paulo, with her parents and her two brothers.

Listen and understand

1 c **2** e **3** b

Test yourself

1a marido **b** pais **c** solteiros **d** mãe **2a** False **b** False **c** True **d** True **e** False **3** 12 16 22 38 85 74 **4a** Você é casada? **b** Quantos anos você tem? **c** Você tem filhos? **d** Ele é muito alto! **e** Onde ele estuda?

UNIT 3

A cozinha brasileira

It means: Joana's black bean stew is excellent.

Vocabulary builder

Drinks/Food mineral, wine, milk, sandwich, chocolate

Conversation 1

1 draught beer **2a** passion fruit, banana and lemon juice **b** fried cassava **c** afternoon / early evening **3 Jorge:** Boa tarde. Um bauru, um x-búrguer e uma porção de mandioca frita. **Mariana:** Um suco de maracujá, banana e limão, e um chope. Obrigada.

Language discovery 1

1 quer / quero / posso? **2** very **3** gosto

Practice 1

1a posso **b** quer **c** deveria **d** devem **2a** realmente **b** bastante **c** um pouco **d** muito **3a** bons **b** má **c** bom **d** mau **4a** likes chocolate **b** hates wine **c** can't stand eggs

Conversation 2

1 tomato salad **2a** rice, chips and beetroot salad **b** red house wine **c** pavê

Language discovery 2

1 masculine / feminine **2** divido com você **3** grelhado / fritas

Practice 2

1a da **b** de **c** de **d** dos **e** da **2a** Divido com você. **b** Quero meu café sem açúcar, por favor. **c** Duas cervejas e uma água sem gás, por favor. **d** Tem pratos sem gluten? **3a** 3 **b** 4 **c** 1 **d** 2

Listen and understand

Márcia wants a salad and a salmon sandwich. **Guilherme** wants rump steak, rice, beans and chips.

Reading and writing

1 adoro / comida / favorito / peixe / adoramos **2a** True **b** True **c** False

Test yourself

1a não **b** vegano **c** alérgica **d** vegetarianos **e** com **f** glúten **2** Silvana orders starter: beetroot salad, main and accompaniment: grilled fish with rice and chips, dessert: lemon mousse, drink: espresso **3 You:** Bom dia. Uma salada César e uma fatia do quiche de espinafre e (***or** com*) queijo. / Um suco de laranja com acerola por favor.

REVIEW 1

1 a sou **b** têm **c** está **d** somos **e** tem **f** estão **2a** Onde você trabalha? **b** O Fernando come peixe? **c** Quando vocês partem? **d** Você gosta de cerveja? **e** Eles vendem queijo? **3a** Ele é alto. **b** Esta comida é muito picante. **c** Ela tem olhos verdes. **d** A sopa está fria. **e** Os sucos são deliciosos. **f** Nós somos vegetarianos. **4a** marido / 57 / seis / março **b** filha / 19 / quinze / junho **c** tia / 72 / vinte e um / setembro **d** primo / 6 / trinta / novembro **e** avó / 91 / dois / maio. The youngest is the cousin. The oldest is the grandmother. The aunt's birthday is in September. **6 You:** no starter/main – frango grelhado / dessert – pavê de abacaxi / drink – caipirinha. **Samuel:** starter – salada de palmito / main – frango grelhado / dessert – salada de frutas OR no dessert / drink – cerveja. **Patrícia:** starter – salada de palmito OR canja / main – ovos recheados OR salada César / dessert – sorvete / drink – suco. **7** (sample answers): **a** Vou bem. **b** Eu me chamo/chamo-me Bob. **c** Trabalho num supermercado. **d** Sim, falo francês bem. **e** Moro em Liverpool. **f** O meu email é... / Tenho or não tenho Instagram. **g** O número do meu celular é 000777444. **h** Sou de Berlim. **i** Não, sou divorciado. **j** Sim, tenho dois filhos. **k** Tenho 35 anos. **l** Faço anos em agosto. **8 Maria:** Lisbon / Portuguese / doctor / married / 0753-00218. **Bruno:** Brazilian (but he and family are from Italy) / Brasília / student / Portuguese, Italian, Spanish / 0371-4825555. **9** Boa noite! Para começar, uns bolinhos de bacalhau / O que recomenda? / Prefiro peixe. / Está bem OR tudo bem. / Uma cerveja, por favor. E uma garrafa de água mineral com gás por favor. / Um mousse de chocolate, por favor. / Sim, obrigado(a). E a conta, por favor.

UNIT 4

Rotinas típicas

In the morning I drink a cup of coffee and eat two pieces of toast with butter before going to work.

Vocabulary builder

Frequency morning, night, rarely **Countries** France, Germany

Conversation 1

1 No, in France he teaches only in the morning **2a** False – he IS enjoying his visit **b** True **c** True

Language discovery 1

1 gostando **2** no – m / f **3** conhecer / sei

Practice 1

1a estou aprendendo **b** estão gostando **c** estou trabalhando **d** estamos fazendo **2a** na **b** nas **c** no **d** em **e** nos **3a** 3 **b** 1 **c** 4 **d** 2

Conversation 2

1 Gabriela yes, Sérgio rarely **2a** 7 hours a day **b** the gym **c** Wednesdays **d** normally at the weekend

Language discovery 2

1 myself **2** me divirto muito **3** segunda

Practice 2

1a se **b** me **c** nos **d** se **2** se / nos / se **3a** 3ª visitar amigos. **b** 5ª trabalhar. **c** sáb. Fazer compras.

Reading and writing

1a Ele está lendo o jornal. **b** Ela está jogando futebol. **c** Ela está vendo televisão. **d** Ele está nadando. **2** viajando / gostando / passando / comprando **3a** estou passando **b** estamos visitando **c** estamos gastando **d** está comendo **e** estão vendo

Listen and understand

a She gets up early, makes breakfast and takes the kids to school. **b** On Wednesdays. **c** On Monday and Wednesday. **d** On Tuesday and Thursday. **e** At home.

Go further

Eduardo Guedes is a famous chef in Brazil. He is from São Paulo. He presents a food programme on a TV channel from Monday to Friday. Sometimes he leaves the studio and travels to various parts of Brazil, preparing delicious dishes from different states and regions. We can see the recipes and the videos on the internet.

Test yourself

1a Portugal **b** Espanha **c** China **d** Canadá **e** França **2a** trabalhar / 35 horas por semana. **b** ir na academia / muitas vezes **c** preparar o café da manhã / geralmente não **d** ir à igreja / todos os domingos **3a** Trabalho trinta horas por semana. **b** Nas sextas janto fora. **c** Eu me levanto cedo. **d** Sempre faço exercício nos sábados.

UNIT 5

Transportes no Brasil

'stopping for 25 minutes'

Vocabulary builder

Travel information ticket, student, last

Conversation 1

1 8 hours 45 minutes **2a** 8.30 p.m. **b** Saturday **c** student card

Language discovery 1
1 A que horas **2** vinte e trinta / oito e meia da noite **3** duzentos e setenta e cinco

Translation of sentence:
I have 3 houses, 30 bills and 300 problems!

Practice 1
1a começa / show **b** chega / ônibus **c** parte / avião **d** abre / banco **2a** 7:50 **b** 11:30 **c** 1:40 **d** 4:15 **e** 8:50 **3a** cento e vinte e seis **b** quatrocentos e noventa e um **c** oitocentos e trinta e dois **d** setecentos e setenta e cinco **e** trezentos e noventa
4 The correct order is: 232 970 681 599 242

Conversation 2
1 platform 5 **2a** True **b** True **c** False **d** True **e** False

Language discovery 2
1 para / para **2** Ser (são) **3** está vindo

Practice 2
1a para **b** por **c** pelo **d** pelo **e** pela **2** levanto / arrumo / bebo / como / tomo / vou **3a** vou **b** vamos **c** vem **d** vêm **e** vão

Reading and writing
1a vai / carro **b** vou / bicicleta **c** vamos / avião **d** vão / pé **e** vamos / trem **2** Há / Tem ônibus para Belo Horizonte de manhã? / Quanto é / custa o ônibus leito? / Quero / Queria duas passagens para sexta-feira de manhã. **3a** São oito horas. **b** São nove e vinte e cinco **c** São três e meia

Listen and understand
1a at 8:15 a.m. **b** at 11 a.m. **c** at 3 p.m. **d** at 6:30 p.m.

Go further
1a four **b** 1 p.m. **c** behind **d** same **2a** 3 **b** 3

Test yourself
1 às / da / no / pode / pegar / para / de **2a** 3 **b** 1 **c** 4 **d** 2 **3a** 11:10 **b** Copacabana **c** 12

UNIT 6

No centro da cidade

250 is the number of the building in Cabo Frio Avenue. He lives in apartment number 602. Jardim Alvorada is the name of the **bairro** *(district)*. 860620-630 is the postcode. Londrina is the name of the city. PR is the abbreviation of the state name, Paraná.

Vocabulary builder

City center market, centre, traffic **Directions** front, far (off / away)

Conversation 1

1 Republic Square **2a** she has to turn left here **b** go to the square and ask again **c** can she see that set of traffic lights over there?

Language discovery 1

1 à esquerda **2** pode / poderia – one means 'can you', the other means 'could you' **3** passar / cruzar

Practice 1

1a à **b** aos **c** às **d** ao **2a** você pode me indicar / mostrar no mapa? **b** você pode repetir por favor? **c** você poderia me trazer o cardápio? **d** você pode me ajudar? **3a** Tem Uber aqui na cidade? OR Aqui na cidade tem Uber? **b** Posso fazer a reserva online? **c** Posso fazer a reserva pelo site? **d** Vocês entregam a comida em casa? **4** the correct order is c / a / b

Conversation 2

1 second floor **2a** no, she doesn't know **b** a bookshop **c** go and see what films are on at the cinema

Language discovery 2

1 neste **2** vire instead of vira – vire is the direct command 'turn!'; vira means 'you turn' **3** at / to the, of the **4** pertinho

Practice 2

1a nesta **b** nestas **c** naquela **d** naqueles **2a** tome **b** passe **c** vá **d** atravesse **3a** uma lojinha **b** um barzinho **c** uma cidadezinha **d** um cafezinho **4a** livraria Santos **b** correio **c** Central de Informação Turística (CIT)

Listen and understand
a in front of the Machado shoe shop **b** Cross the street and walk in the direction of the park. **c** Turn left. **d** Number 510 **e** Apartment 204

Writing
horas / ponto / leva / chegar / antes

Go further
a emergency exit **b** underground parking **c** lifts **d** cashier **e** no smoking **f** open **g** closed **h** restaurant on the 3rd floor

Test yourself
1a 3 **b** 1 **c** 4 **d** 5 **e** 2 **2a** farmácia **b** avenida **c** direita **d** segunda **e** banco **3a** 2ª **b** 5º **c** 7º **d** 1ª **e** 10ª

REVIEW 2
1a come **b** bebo **c** conhecemos **d** comem **e** bebe **f** conhece **2a** At 6:30 a.m. **b** a piece of bread with cheese and a small cup of coffee **c** on Saturday, at 10:30 a.m. **d** She goes to church with her family and then they have lunch at a 'quilo' restaurant. **3a** em **b** na / no **c** no / de **d** no / de **e** de / na **4a** Ele está bebendo café. **b** Ela está dormindo. **c** Ele está comendo um sanduíche. **d** Ele está lendo um livro. **6** A que horas há/tem ônibus para Petrópolis? / Quanto custa? / Quanto é? / Quanto tempo leva? / Uma passagem de ida e volta, por favor. **7a** Monday **b** 10 reais **c** It is free. **8a** Sabe onde é / fica o Palácio de Cristal? **b** O Palácio de Cristal é longe? **c** Pode me mostrar no mapa? **9** d **10** b, e, a, f, c, d **11a** 410 **b** 550 **c** 178 **d** 925 **e** 233 **12a** 5 **b** 4 **c** 1 **d** 2 **e** 3 **13a** Quando **b** Como **c** Quanto tempo **d** Onde **e** O que

UNIT 7
Alojamento
hotel-fazenda

Vocabulary builder
in the hotel: family / access; **in the room:** air conditioning

Conversation 1
1 Room booked for eight nights **2a** 3 **b** 2 **c** 1 **d** 4

Language discovery 1

1 Como se escreve o seu sobrenome? **2** Quais são os seus nomes? Every word has become plural. **3** partir – usually means to leave **4** de fácil acesso / deserta / movimentada

Practice 1

1a White **b** Pereira **c** Olivetti **2a** fácil **b** hotéis **c** lençóis **d** espanhol **e** azul **3a** O restaurante abre para o almoço ao meio-dia. **b** O café da manhã é servido a partir das seis. **c** Tem música ao vivo todos os sábados. **d** A cidade fica sempre lotada durante o carnaval. **4a** cidade **b** as praias **c** o quarto **d** os apartamentos

Conversation 2

1 the meeting room **2** gym open from 6 a.m. to 11 p.m. **3a** left **b** underground / under the hotel **c** it's dirty and needs to be cleaned **d** at any time

Language discovery 2

1 chegar / acabar – to finish **2** there's a booklet missing – falta um livrinho **3** reunião **4** fechada / suja

Practice 2

1a 3 **b** 4 **c** 1 **d** 2 **2a** a towel **b** information **c** sheets **d** milk **e** three plates **3a** aviões / avião **b** estações / estação **c** órgãos / órgão **4a** estou cansada **b** está frio **c** estão abertas **d** estamos tristes

Reading and listening

1 walking and bicycle rides **2** 60 rooms **3** delicious fish dishes **4** sauna / squash / tennis **5** c **6** a **7** c

Reading

a 3 **b** 4 **c** 2 **d** 1

Go further

Typical check-in information:

Nome: Mary	Sobrenome: Jones
Data de nascimento : 23/09/1984	Local de nascimento: Christ church, Nova Zelândia
Número da Identidade/passaporte: 0987BZMJ1178	
Endereço: 23 Market Street, Glasgow, Escócia, GL45 6NH	
E-mail: newscot84@hello.com	
Telefone celular: 01102030405	

Test yourself

1a O chuveiro não funciona. **b** A que horas abre o bar? **c** Qual é o código / a senha do wifi? **d** Pode chamar um táxi para nós? **2a** solteiro. **b** três / 3 **c** Martin **d** 56 **3a** Tenho uma reserva. **b** Temos um quarto / um apartamento reservado para cinco noites. **c** A que horas servem o café da manhã? **d** O quarto / O apartamento tem cofre?

UNIT 8

Fazendo compras

The sign means 'sale – 40% discount on items paid for there and then or by instalments'

Vocabulary builder

Clothing / clothes blouse, sandals **Colors** white, green, beige

Conversation 1

1 black blouse **2a** 65 reais each **b** over there on the left **c** Vanda's skirt

Language discovery 1

1 uma blusa preta / uma blusa branca **2** aquelas ali **3** cara / mais barata / as mais bonitas – all are feminine to agree with blusa

Practice 1

1a verde **b** amarelas **c** marrons **d** roxa **2a** este vestido aqui **b** aquelas camisetas ali **c** esse relógio aí **d** estes cintos aqui **3** nova / fresca / mais /o mais

Conversation 2

1 a pair of flip-flops in orange and blue **2** Música Popular Brasileira (Brazilian pop music) **3a** False **b** False **c** True

Language discovery 2

1 lindíssimas / baratíssimos **2** Que tal ...? **3** vinte e cinco mil / quarenta e oito mil **4** dá-me / me dê

Practice 2

1a apertadíssimos **b** baratíssimas **c** certíssima **d** chatíssimo **e** caríssimos **2a** a small towel **b** the bag in green **c** why not buy five? **3a** 2.518 **b** 1975 **c** 36.400 **d** 1.089 **e** 72.462 **4** me telefona / me manda / me conta

Reading

1a 6 **b** 1 **c** 6 **d** 1 **e** 4 **f** 8 **g** 7 **h** 2 **i** 8 **j** 4 **k** 5

Listen and understand

1 short-sleeved **2** large **3** white

Test yourself

1a Havaianas **b** Relógio **c** Sapatos **d** Terno **e** Vestido **2a** True **b** False **c** False **d** True

UNIT 9

Celebrações

Invitation to: a christening, birthday, 15th birthday party, wedding

Vocabulary builder

Holidays: week, Carnival, Independence **Activities:** to visit the family

Conversation 1

1 by spending a few hours at the club **2a** staying in the swimming pool **b** her nephew's christening **c** the next weekend

Language discovery 1

1 tô (estou) pensando/estávamos pensando **2** formal: conosco / informal: com a gente **3** it makes it seem larger **4** fim de semana, amendoim

Practice 1

1a 3 **b** 4 **c** 1 **d** 5 **e** 2 **2a** com eles **b** comigo **c** com a gente **d** contigo **3a** gatão **b** um tempão **c** um garrafão **d** cachorrão **e** beijão **f** abração **4** jardins; mensagens; som; bombons; nuvem

Conversation 2

1 8 days **2a** he says it's worth it – beach, sun, beer ... **b** going to New York with Cecília **c** she can't wait

Language discovery 2

1 faz um tempão que não vou para a praia **2** vem comigo **3** gostaria **4** so good / tão barato

Practice 2

1a True **b** False **c** True **d** True **2a** Arthur, come with us! **b** Take your change! **c** Come and see the new shopping centre! **d** Carla, listen to my message and answer me! **3a** 3 **b** 4 **c** 2 **d** 1 **4a** tão **b** tanto **c** tantos **d** tão

Reading

1 Ela vai à festa junina no Parque da Cidade. **2** Ela vai encontrar os pais dela. **3** A festa de aniversário do Carlos é na sexta-feira. **4** Ela vai à/na praia no sábado de manhã. **5** Ela vai ao campeonato de vôlei de praia.

Listen and understand

1 A barbecue **2** His wife and daughter. **3** Next Sunday

Writing

(sample answer): Oi Jorge! Obrigado pelo convite para o churrasco. Seria ótimo, mas não vai dar certo – vamos passar o domingo na praia. Parabéns! Tchau! Ricardo.

Go further

Birthday song: happy birthday (congratulations) to you, on this dear date, many joys (much happiness), many years of life!

Test yourself

1a domingo **b** trabalhar **c** dá certo **d** irmão **2a** 2 **b** 5 **c** 1 **d** 4 **e** 3 **3a** Você tem planos para o feriado? **b** Vou passar o fim de semana no litoral. **c** Obrigado(a) pelo convite! **d** Gostaria de visitar Brasília. **e** Mal posso esperar!

UNIT 10

Lazer

The best time to visit the amusement park is in low season.

Vocabulary builder

Sports and leisure to relax, to dance, theatre **Past tense** visit

Conversation 1

1a It was great! **2a** 3 **b** 1 **c** 4 **d** 2

Language discovery 1
1 todo o mundo gostou; recebeu o cartão vermelho; eles começaram mal **2** I didn't see / watch; I couldn't; I went **3** ótimo, interessantíssimo; foi

Practice 1
1a relaxei **b** perdeu **c** assistiram **d** visitamos **e** desapareceu **2a** 1 **b** 2 **c** 2 **3a** great **b** marvellous **c** awful **d** funny

Conversation 2
1 a bag and two skirts **2a** visiting family **b** a show in the square **c** to catch the bus **d** She slept a lot, stayed at home and watched films on Netflix.

Language discovery 2
1 Não fiz nada / tive que voltar / gerente de mídia digital **2** ficar **3** no fim de semana / no sábado / no domingo; na terça-feira

Practice 2
1a fiz **b** tiveram **c** disse **d** fizemos **e** teve **2a** joguei **b** explicou **c** brinquei **d** pagou **e** cheguei **3a** A semana passada eu joguei basquete. **b** Ontem fomos ao teatro. **c** O filme terminou às nove e trinta. **d** Na quinta-feira ela foi à academia.

Reading and writing
1a False **b** True **c** False **d** True **2** no / cara / dentro / tanto / dormir

Listen and understand
João: His house was robbed. They took the TV, the computer and some clothes. It happened at the weekend. **Carolina:** She lost her wallet at the shopping centre this afternoon. It had a credit card and 150 reais in it. **Jair:** His dog Guga disappeared yesterday morning.

Go further
resolveram / venderam / compraram / realizaram

Test yourself
1 Correct order: ir fazer compras / encontrar Ana / ir ao cinema / ficar em casa / ver TV / passar a manhã no clube / assistir um show **2** ontem / uma boate / voltei / Adorei! / ótimo **3** (sample answers): **a** Ontem fui fazer compras. **b** No sábado fui à praia. **c** Sim, gostei muito. **d** O jogo foi ruim. **e** Visitei a Espanha.

REVIEW 3

1a 4 **b** 1 **c** 2 **d** 5 **e** 3 **2** Boa tarde. / Tenho uma reserva; um quarto de solteiro reservado para três noites. / (sample answer) Sandra Brown. / (sample answer) B-R-O-W-N. / Aqui. / A que horas servem o café da manhã? / Obrigado(a). **3a** shower doesn't work **b** there aren't any towels **c** the plate's dirty **d** there's a lot of noise **e** there's no internet access **4a** ao meio-dia **b** hóspede **c** preço **d** tamanho **e** comer **5a** saiu dançar / com o amigo **b** no sábado passado/toda a família **c** em agosto / foi a um concerto de música rock **d** relaxou no clube / o namorado. **e** durante as férias da Páscoa / viajaram para o litoral **7** Eu queria esta camisa do Brasil em G (tamanho grande), por favor. / Prefiro com manga curta. Quanto é? / Também queria um chapéu de sol / praia. / Então vou levar um. Posso experimentar a camisa? / Que pena! Obrigado(a). **8a** False **b** True **c** False **d** True **e** False **f** False **9** missing words: piscina tropical / jogar / fazer / pescar / fazer / bar **10a** Luxury apartments at country hotel **b** nature trails, waterfalls, lakes **c** coffee, juices and little cheese breads / balls **d** in the bar **e** light meals, tea and cakes, variety of national and international drinks

Portuguese–English glossary

Words and expressions appear in the glossary with the meaning they have in the context of this course; it is often the case that expressions have a variety of meanings, depending on how they are used. A good dictionary is indispensable for improving your all-round language acquisition.

abacaxi (m)	*pineapple*
aberto(a)	*open*
abertura (f)	*opening (hours)*
abração (m)	*big hug*
abrir	*to open*
absurdo(a)	*absurd*
acabar	*to end / finish*
acabar de ...	*to have just ...*
academia (f)	*gym*
açaí (m)	*açaí berry*
acampar	*to go camping*
acarajé (m)	*black-eyed pea fritter*
acerola (f)	*acerola berry*
acesso (m)	*access*
achar	*to find / think*
acompanhamento (m)	*accompaniment / side dish*
aconselhar	*to advise*
acontecer	*to happen*
acreditar	*to believe*
adeus	*goodbye*
adorar	*to love / adore*
aeroporto (m)	*airport*
agora	*now*
agradável	*pleasant*
água mineral (f)	*mineral water*
aguardente (f)	*another name for* **cachaça**, *a sugar cane spirit similar to white rum*
ah é?	*is that so? / really?*

aí	*there / and then*
ajuda (f)	*help*
ajudar	*to help*
Alemanha (f)	*Germany*
alemão(ã)	*German*
alérgico(a) (a / ao)	*allergic (to)*
algodão (m)	*cotton*
alguns / algumas (m pl / f pl)	*some / any*
ali	*over there*
aliás	*what's more*
alimentação (f)	*food*
alívio	*relief;* **que alívio!** *what a relief!*
almoço (m)	*lunch*
alto(a)	*tall*
aluno(a) (m / f)	*school pupil*
amanhã	*tomorrow*
amarelo(a)	*yellow*
ameixa (f)	*plum*
amendoim torrado (m)	*roasted peanut*
americano(a)	*American*
amigo(a) (m / f)	*friend*
andar	*to walk*
andar (m)	*floor*
aniversário (m)	*birthday / anniversary*
antes (de)	*before*
ao lado (de)	*next to*
ao / à / aos / às	*to the / at the*
apartamento (m)	*apartment / flat / room (in hotel)*
apertado(a)	*tight*
aquele(a)	*that (one)*
aqui	*here*
árabe	*Arabic*
ar-condicionado (m)	*air conditioning*
árbitro (m)	*referee*
armário (m)	*cupboard / wardrobe*
arroz doce (m)	*sweet rice / rice pudding*
arrumar-se	*to get dressed; to get ready*
assado(a)	*roasted*
assim	*in this way / and so*

assinar	*to sign*
assistente social	*social worker*
assistir	*to watch / attend*
até	*until / up to*
até amanhã	*see you tomorrow*
até de noite	*even at night / see you tonight*
até logo	*see you later*
até mais tarde	*see you later on*
atrações (f pl)	*attractions / entertainment*
atrás (de)	*behind*
atrasado(a)	*late*
atravessar	*to cross (over)*
aula (f)	*lesson*
australiano(a)	*Australian*
automóvel	*car*
avenida (f)	*avenue*
aviação (f) **curso de** (m)	*aviation / flying course*
avião (m)	*aeroplane;* **por avião** *by air*
azeite (m)	*(olive) oil*
azul	*blue*
azul turquesa	*turquoise*
bairro (m)	*district / neighborhood*
baixo(a)	*short / low*
bagunça (f)	*mess*
banana (f)	*banana*
banheira (f)	*bathtub*
banheiro (m)	*bathroom*
bar (m)	*bar*
barato(a)	*cheap*
barba (f)	*beard*
barca (f)	*boat / ferry*
barco (m)	*boat / ferry*
barulhento(a)	*noisy*
barulho (m)	*noise*
basquete (m)	*basketball*
bastante	*quite / enough*
batatas fritas (f pl)	*chips*
batida (f)	*cocktail*
batida (f) **de côco**	*coconut cocktail*

batizado (m)	*christening*
bauru (m)	*sandwich made with French bread, containing roast beef or ham, tomatoes, pickles and melted cheese*
beber	*to drink*
bebida (f)	*drink*
bege	*beige*
beijo (m)	*kiss*
beleza!	*fantastic!*
bem	*well / well then;* **tudo bem?** *is everything OK?;* **tudo bem** *everything's OK*
bengala (f)	*walking stick*
beterraba (f)	*beetroot*
bicicleta (f)	*bicycle*
bigode (m)	*moustache*
bilhete (m)	*ticket*
biodiversidade (f)	*biodiversity*
biquíni (m)	*bikini*
blusa (f)	*blouse*
boa estada! / boa estadia!	*have a nice stay!*
boa noite	*good evening / goodnight*
boa tarde	*good afternoon / good evening*
boa viagem!	*bon voyage!*
boas férias!	*have a good holiday!*
boate (f)	*nightclub*
bolo (m) **(de limão)**	*(lemon) cake*
bolsa (f)	*bag*
bom dia	*good morning / hello*
bom / boa / bons / boas	*good*
bombom (pl **bombons**) (m)	*sweet*
bonitinho(a)	*pretty / cute*
botas (f pl)	*boots*
branco(a)	*white*
Brasil (m)	*Brazil*
brigar	*to argue / fight*
brincar	*to play*
cabelos (m pl)	*hair*
cachaça (f)	*sugar cane spirit similar to white rum*
cachoeira (f)	*waterfall*

cachorro (m) *dog*
cada *each*
cadeira de rodas (f) *wheelchair*
café (m) *café / coffee*
café (m) **com leite** *white coffee*
café (m) **da manhã** *breakfast*
cafezinho (m) *a small black coffee, similar to an espresso*
caipirinha (f) *cocktail made from cachaça, lime juice, sugar and crushed ice*
caixa (f) *box / check out*
caixa automático (m) *ATM / cash machine*
calça (f) *trousers*
calçadão (m) *promenade*
calmo(a) *calm*
cama (f) *bed*
camarões (m pl) *shrimps*
caminhada (f) *walk / stroll*
caminho *way;* **a caminho para** *on the way to*
camisa (f) *shirt*
camiseta (f) *T-shirt*
Canadá (m) *Canada*
canal (m) **de televisão** *TV channel*
canja (f) *chicken broth*
cansado(a) *tired*
canto (m) *corner (inside)*
cardápio (m) *menu*
careca *bald*
Carnaval (m) *Carnival*
carne assada (f) *roast meat*
carne de sol (f) *sundried meat*
caro(a) *expensive*
carro(m) *car*
carta (f) *letter*
cartão (m) *card*
carteira (f) *wallet / purse / card*
carteira (f) **de estudante** *student card*
carteira (f) **de identidade** *ID card*
casa (f) *house;* **em casa** *at home*

casado(a)	*married*
casamento (m)	*wedding*
castanho(a)	*brown (hair / eyes)*
castelo (m)	*castle*
catedral (f)	*cathedral*
cavalo (m)	*horse*
cê = você	*you*
cedo	*early*
cenoura (f)	*carrot*
Central (f) **de Informação Turística (CIT)**	*tourist information center*
centro (m) **da cidade**	*city center*
Centro (m) **de Convenções**	*conference center*
centro (m) **financeiro e comercial**	*financial and commercial center*
centro (m) **cultural**	*cultural center*
certo	*of course / certainly / right*
cerveja (f)	*beer*
cetim (m)	*satin*
chá (m) **(com leite)**	*tea (with milk)*
chamar-se	*to be called*
chapéu (m)	*hat*
chato(a)	*boring / annoying*
chegar	*to arrive*
cheio(a)	*full*
chinês(a)	*Chinese*
chope (m)	*draught beer*
churrascaria (f)	*steak house*
churrasco (m)	*barbecue*
chuveiro (m)	*shower (in bathroom)*
cidade (f)	*town / city*
cigarro (m)	*cigarette*
cima: em cima (de)	*on top (of)*
cinema (m)	*cinema*
cinto (m)	*belt*
cinza	*grey*
claro(a)	*clear / light*
clube (m)	*leisure center*
código (m)	*code, password*
cofre (m)	*safe deposit box*

coisa (f)	*thing*
com	*with*
com certeza	*certainly*
com licença	*excuse me*
combinar	*to go with / match*
começar	*to start / begin*
comer	*to eat*
comida (baiana / mineira) (f)	*food (from Bahia / Minas)*
comida (f) **por quilo**	*food sold by weight*
comissário(a) de bordo	*flight attendant*
complicado(a)	*complicated*
compras	*shopping;* **fazer compras** *to go shopping*
comum/ns (sing / pl)	*common*
concordar	*to agree*
concurso (m) **público**	*civil service exam*
conhecer	*to know (person / place)*
conosco	*with us*
consultório (m)	*surgery / consultation room*
conta (f)	*bill;* **por conta própria** *on one's own*
contar	*to count*
contente	*happy / content*
convenção (f)	*conference*
convencional	*standard class / conventional*
convidado (m)	*guest (at party, etc.)*
convite (m)	*invitation*
cor (f)	*color*
coragem (f)	*courage*
cor-de-rosa	*pink*
coreano(a)	*Korean*
correio (m)	*post office*
correr	*to run*
couro (m)	*leather*
coxinha (f)	*large deep-fried chicken and potato croquette*
cozido(a)	*boiled*
cozinha (f)	*kitchen*
cozinheiro(a) (m / f)	*cook*
criador(a) de conteúdo	*content creator*

crianças (f pl) **(de colo)** — *children (lit. on lap / babies who still haven't learned to walk)*

cru / crua — *raw*

cruzar — *to cross*

cuidador(a) — *carer*

cultura (f) — *culture*

curto(a) — *short*

custar — *to cost*

daí — *and then / and so*

dançar — *to dance*

dar — *to give*

dar certo — *to turn out OK*

dar para — *to be possible*

data (f) **de nascimento** — *date of birth*

de / do / da / dos / das — *of (the) / from (the)*

debaixo (de) — *under / underneath*

decepcionado(a) — *disappointed*

decidir — *to decide*

décimo(a) — *tenth*

deixar — *to leave / let*

demais — *too (much)*

demorar — *to take a long time*

dentista (m / f) — *dentist*

dentro (de) — *inside / within*

depois (de) — *after / afterwards*

desaparecer — *to disappear*

descer — *to go down*

desconto (m) — *discount*

desculpe — *sorry / excuse me*

designer gráfico — *graphic designer*

despertador (m) — *alarm clock*

destino (m) — *destination*

detestar — *to hate / detest*

Deus me livre! — *God forbid!*

devagar — *slowly*

dever — *to have to / owe*

devolver — *to return (give back)*

dia (m) — *day;* **o dia todo** *all day;* **todos os dias** *every day*

Dia (m) **da Independência**	*Independence Day*
Dia (m) **da Proclamação da República**	*Day of the Proclamation of the Republic*
diário(a)	*daily*
diferente	*different*
difícil / difíceis (sing / pl)	*difficult*
dinheiro (m)	*money*
direções (f pl)	*directions*
direita	*right;* **à direita** *on / to the right*
direto(a)	*straight / direct*
divertido(a)	*funny / enjoyable*
divertir-se	*to enjoy oneself*
dividir	*to divide / share*
divorciado(a)	*divorced*
dizer	*to say / tell*
doce	*sweet*
domingo (m)	*Sunday*
dormir	*to sleep*
dublado	*dubbed*
durante	*during*
e	*and*
e daí?	*and so? / so what?*
e tal	*and so on / and whatever*
economia (f)	*economy / economics*
edifício (m)	*building*
ele / ela	*he / she / it*
eles / elas	*they*
eletricista (m / f)	*electrician*
eletrodomésticos (m pl)	*household appliances*
elevador (m)	*lift*
email (m)	*email*
embalagem (f)	*package*
empregada (f)	*maid*
empregado(a) (m / f)	*employee / clerk*
emprego (m)	*job*
empresa (f)	*business*
encanador(ora) (m / f)	*plumber*
encontrar	*to meet / find*
endereço (m)	*address*
engarrafamento (m)	*traffic jam*

engraçado(a)	*funny / amusing*
enorme	*huge*
enquanto	*while*
ensino médio (m)	*secondary school education*
então	*then / well then / in that case*
enteado(a)	*stepson / stepdaughter*
entender	*to understand*
entrada (f)	*entrance*
entregar	*to hand over / deliver*
entrevista (f)	*interview*
época (f) **seca / de chuva**	*dry / rainy season*
escada rolante	*escalator*
Escócia (f)	*Scotland*
escola (f) **primária**	*primary school*
escolher	*to choose*
escrever	*to write*
escritório (m)	*office*
escuro(a)	*dark*
escutar	*to listen (to)*
esfirra (f)	*Lebanese-style bread cake with minced meat filling (esfiha)*
Espanha (f)	*Spain*
espanhol(a)	*Spanish*
especial	*special*
especialidade (f) **da casa**	*house speciality*
esperar	*to wait / hope*
esperto(a)	*smart*
espinafre (f)	*spinach*
esporte (m)	*sport*
esposa (f)	*wife*
esposo (m)	*husband*
esquerda	*left;* **à esquerda** *on / to the left*
esquina (f)	*corner (street)*
estação (f)	*station*
estacionamento (grátis) (m)	*(free) parking*
Estados Unidos (m pl)	*USA*
estar	*to be*
estar com calor / frio	*to be hot / cold*
estar com fome / sede	*to be hungry / thirsty*

estar com pressa	*to be in a hurry*
este / esta (m / f)	*this (one)*
estilo (m)	*style*
estrada (f)	*road*
estrelas (f pl)	*stars*
eu	*I*
evento (m)	*event*
exatamente	*exactly*
executivo	*luxury standard*
experimentar	*to try on*
explicar	*to explain*
extra grande	*extra large*
fácil	*easy;* **de fácil acesso** *easily accessible*
faculdade (f)	*faculty (university)*
falador(ora)	*talkative*
falar	*to speak / talk*
falta (f) **de (educação)**	*lack of (good manners)*
faltar	*to be lacking / missing*
família (f)	*family*
fantasma (m)	*ghost*
farmácia (f)	*chemist's*
fazenda (f)	*farm / estate*
fazer	*to do / make*
fechado(a)	*closed*
fechar	*to close*
feijoada (f)	*black bean stew*
feio(a)	*ugly*
feira hippie (f)	*artisan market*
feirinha (f)	*marketplace*
feriado (m)	*bank holiday*
férias (f pl)	*holidays*
festa (f)	*party*
Festa (f) **de Quinze Anos**	*fifteenth birthday party*
Festas Juninas (f pl)	*'June' festivals*
ficar	*to stay / be located / become*
ficha (f)	*form*
ficha (f) **de registro de entrada no hotel**	*hotel check-in form*
filho(a) (m / f)	*son / daughter*
fim (m)	*end*

fim (m) **de semana**	*weekend;* **no fim de semana** *at the weekend*
florido(a)	*flowery*
foto (f)	*photo*
França (f)	*France*
frente	*front;* **em frente (de)** *in front (of) / opposite*
frigobar (m)	*minibar*
frio(a)	*cold*
frito(a)	*fried*
fruta (f)	*fruit*
fumar	*to smoke*
funcionar	*to function / work*
funcionário público (m)	*civil servant*
fusos horários (m pl)	*time zones*
futebol (m)	*football*
galera (f)	*folks, guys;* **oi galera!** *hi guys! / hi folks!*
ganhar	*to win*
garagem (f)	*garage*
garçom / garçonete (m / f)	*server*
garfo (m)	*fork*
garrafa (f)	*bottle*
gás (m)	*gas;* **com / sem gás** *fizzy / still (drinks)*
gastar	*to spend*
gato (m)	*cat*
geada (f)	*frost*
gelo (m)	*ice;* **com / sem gelo** *with / without ice*
gengibre (m)	*ginger*
genro (m)	*son in law*
Gente!	*You guys!*
gentil/is (sing / pl)	*kind*
geralmente	*generally*
gerente (m / f)	*manager*
gordo(a)	*fat*
gorjeta (f)	*tip*
gostar (de)	*to like*
gostoso(a)	*tasty / nice*
grande	*large / big*
gravata (f)	*tie*

grego(a) — *Greek*
grelhado(a) — *grilled*
grisalho(a) — *grey (hair)*
guaraná (m) — *refreshing fizzy drink made with the Amazonian fruit of the same name*

há — *there is / are*
hambúrguer (m) — *hamburger*
havaianas (f pl) — *famous Brazilian flip-flop brand*
hoje — *today*
homem (pl **homens**) (m) — *man / men*
hora (f) — *hour / time;* **a qualquer hora** *at any time*
horário (m) — *timetable*
horrível — *horrible*
hortelã (f) — *mint*
hóspede (m) — *guest*
hospital (pl **hospitais**) (m) — *hospital*
hotel (pl **hotéis**) (m) — *hotel*
hotel-fazenda (m) — *country hotel*
ida: de ida — *single;* **de ida e volta** *return*
ideia — *idea*
idoso(a) — *old / aged / elderly*
igreja (f) — *church*
ilha (f) — *island*
importar-se — *to mind / care*
incomodar — *to disturb / bother*
indicar — *to indicate / show*
infelizmente — *unfortunately*
influenciador(a) — *influencer*
Inglaterra (f) — *England*
inglês(a) — *English*
ingresso (m) — *entrance ticket*
inteirinho(a) — *complete / whole*
inteligente — *clever*
intercâmbio (m) — *exchange programme*
interessar — *to interest*
interior (m) — *interior (inland) / countryside*
inverno (m) — *winter*
ir — *to go*
irmão(ã) (m / f) — *brother / sister*

italiano(a)	*Italian*
já	*already / now*
já que ...	*(seeing) as ...*
janela (f)	*window*
jantar (fora)	*to dine (out)*
japonês(a)	*Japanese*
jaqueta (f)	*jacket*
jardim (pl **jardins**) (m)	*garden*
jeans (m pl)	*jeans*
jeito	*way;* **ter jeito** *to work out OK / to be possible*
jogar	*to play (sport)*
jogo (m)	*game / match*
jornal (pl **jornais**) (m)	*newspaper*
juros	*interest;* **sem juros** *without interest*
lá	*there*
lã (f)	*wool*
ladrão (m)	*thief*
lago (m)	*lake*
lanche (m)	*snack*
lanchonete (f)	*snack bar / café*
laranja (f)	*orange*
lazer (m)	*leisure*
legal!	*brilliant! / great!*
legenda (f)	*subtitle*
lembrança (f)	*souvenir*
lençól (pl **lençóis**) (m)	*sheet*
lentes (f pl) **de contato**	*contact lenses*
ler	*to read*
levantar peso	*to weight-lift*
levantar-se	*to get up*
levar	*to take*
leve	*light (in weight)*
limpar	*to clean*
limpo(a)	*clean*
linguiça (f)	*pork sausage*
linha (f)	*line*
linho (m)	*linen*
liquidação (f)	*sale*

listrado(a)	*striped*
litoral (m)	*coast*
livraria (f)	*bookshop*
livrinho (m) **de informações**	*information booklet*
local (m) **de nascimento**	*place of birth*
loiro(a)	*blonde*
loja (f)	*shop*
loja (f) **de departamentos**	*department store*
longe	*far (off)*
longo(a)	*long*
lotado(a)	*crowded*
lugar (m)	*place*
luxuoso(a)	*luxury*
maçã (f)	*apple*
madrasta (f)	*stepmother*
mãe (f)	*mother*
maiô (m)	*swimsuit*
maior	*larger / greater*
mais	*more*
mais ou menos	*more or less*
mal	*badly*
mala (f)	*suitcase*
mandar	*to send*
mandioca frita (f)	*fried cassava*
manga (f) **comprida / curta**	*long / short sleeved*
manhã (f)	*morning;* **da / de manhã** *in the morning;* **de manhã cedo** *early in the morning*
mão (f)	*hand;* **boa mão** *'good hand' (refers to a good cook);* **má mão** *'bad hand' (refers to a bad cook)*
mapa (m)	*map*
maracujá (m)	*passion fruit*
marido (m)	*husband*
marrom	*brown*
mas	*but*
mau / má / maus / más	*bad*
máximo(a)	*best*
médico(a) (m / f)	*doctor*
médio(a)	*medium*

meia-noite (f)	*midnight*
meias (f pl)	*socks*
meio-dia (m)	*midday*
melhor	*better / best*
menor	*smaller*
menos	*less*
mensagem (f)	*message*
mercado (m)	*market*
mergulhar	*to dive*
metrô (m)	*underground*
meu Deus!	*goodness me! / oh my God!*
meu/s (m / pl)	*my / mine*
mídia (f)	*media*
mil	*(a) thousand*
minha/s (f / pl)	*my / mine*
moça (f)	*girl / lady*
moda (f)	*fashion;* **na moda** *in fashion*
molho (m)	*sauce;* **molho de churrasco / vinagrete / agridoce** *barbecue sauce / vinaigrette / sweet and sour sauce*
momento (m)	*moment*
montanha russa (f)	*rollercoaster*
montão	*pile;* **um montão de ...** *a pile of ...*
monte (m)	*hill*
morango (m)	*strawberry*
morar	*to live*
moreno(a)	*brown / tanned*
mostrar	*to show*
motorista (m / f)	*driver*
mousse (m)	*mousse*
móveis (m pl)	*furniture*
movimentado(a)	*busy (place)*
mudar	*to change*
muitas vezes (f pl)	*many times / often*
muito/a/os/as	*much / many*
muito prazer	*pleased to meet you*
mulher (f)	*wife / woman*
mundo (m)	*world*
museu (m)	*museum*

música (f) **(sertaneja)**	*(country) music*
nada	*nothing*
nadar	*to swim*
namorado(a) (m / f)	*boy / girlfriend*
não	*no / not*
não sei	*I don't know*
naquele / naquela / naqueles / naquelas	*in that / those, on that / those*
Natal (m)	*Christmas*
né?	*isn't it? / aren't you? etc.*
negócio (m)	*business*
neste / nesta / nestes / nestas	*in this / these, on this / these*
neve (f)	*snow*
noite (f)	*night;* **da / de noite** *at night*
nome (m)	*name*
nono(a)	*ninth*
nora (f)	*daughter in law*
normalmente	*normally*
norueguês(a)	*Norwegian*
nós	*we*
nossa!	*wow!*
nosso/a/s (m / f / pl)	*our / ours*
notícias (f pl)	*news*
novela (f)	*soap opera*
novo(a)	*new / young;* **de novo** *again*
noz, nozes (f)	*nut, nuts*
número (m) **de identidade / passaporte**	*ID / passport number*
nunca	*never*
nuvem (pl **nuvens**) (f)	*cloud*
obrigado(a)	*thank you*
óculos (m pl)	*glasses*
odear	*to hate*
oferta (f)	*offer;* **na oferta** *on offer*
oi!	*Hi!*
oitavo(a)	*eighth*
olhar	*to look*
olhos (m pl)	*eyes*
onde?	*where?*
ônibus (m)	*bus;* **ônibus leito** *sleeper bus (with reclining seats)*

ontem	*yesterday*
ótimo!	*great! / brilliant!*
ótimo(a)	*great / best*
ou	*or*
outra vez (f)	*again*
ouvir	*to hear / listen to*
ovo (m)	*egg*
ovos recheados (m pl)	*stuffed eggs*
pacote (m)	*package*
padaria (f)	*bakery*
padrasto (m)	*stepfather*
pagar	*to pay*
pai (m)	*father*
país (m)	*country*
paisagem (f)	*countryside*
palmito (m)	*heart of palm*
pão (m)	*bread*
papel (pl **papéis**) (m)	*paper*
par (m)	*pair*
para	*for / to / in order to*
para mim	*for me*
parabéns!	*Congratulations!*
parada (f)	*stop (bus)*
parecer	*to seem*
parede (f)	*wall (of building)*
parque (m)	*park*
partir	*to leave / break;* **a partir de** *... from ... (time)*
Páscoa (f)	*Easter*
passagem (f)	*ticket (for travel)*
passar	*to pass / spend (time)*
pavê (m) **de abacaxi**	*creamy biscuit tart with pineapple*
pé (m)	*foot*
peça (f)	*piece*
pechincha!	*bargain!*
pedaço (m)	*bit / piece*
pedir	*to ask (for)*
pegar	*to get / grab / catch*
peixe (m)	*fish*
pena	*pity;* **que pena!** *what a shame / pity!*

pensar	*to think*
pequeno(a)	*small*
perder	*to lose*
perfil (m)	*profile*
perigoso(a)	*dangerous*
perfumaria (f)	*perfume shop / perfume counter*
pergunta (f)	*question*
perguntar	*to ask (question)*
perrengue (m)	*unexpected trouble, difficulty* (slang)
pertinho	*really close*
perto	*near / close*
pescar	*to fish*
pesquisa (f)	*survey*
péssimo(a)	*awful*
pessoas (f pl)	*people*
pessoas com deficiência	*disabled people*
pessoas com mobilidade reduzida	*people with reduced mobility*
picanha (f) **com feijão**	*rump steak with black beans*
picante	*spicy*
pimenta (m)	*chilli*
pinga (f)	*another name for* **cachaça**, *a sugar cane spirit similar to white rum*
pipoca (f)	*popcorn*
piscina (f)	*swimming pool*
plataforma (f)	*platform*
poder	*to be able / know how to*
pois não?	*can I help you?*
política (f)	*politics*
poluído(a)	*polluted*
ponto (m) **de ônibus**	*bus stop*
por	*per*
por avião / estrada	*by air / road*
por conta própria	*on one's own*
por mês / semana / ano	*per month / week / year*
porção (f)	*portion*
porcaria (f)	*mess / rubbish*
porco (m) **grelhado**	*grilled pork*
porque	*because*
porta (f)	*door*

portão (m)	*gate*
porto (m)	*port*
Portugal	*Portugal*
possível	*possible*
poucas vezes (f pl)	*not often / seldom*
pousada (f)	*hotel*
praça (f)	*square (town)*
praça (f) **de alimentação**	*food hall*
praia (f)	*beach*
praticar	*to practice*
prato (m)	*plate / dish*
prato principal (m)	*main course*
prazo	*time limit;* **à prazo** *in instalments*
precisar	*to need*
preço (m)	*price*
prédio (m) **de apartamentos**	*block of flats*
preencher	*to fill in (form)*
preferir	*to prefer*
pregado/a	*worn out / tired* (slang)
preocupar-se	*to worry*
presente (m)	*present / gift*
presunto (m)	*ham*
preto(a)	*black*
previsto(a)	*forecast / expected*
primeiro(a)	*first*
primo/a (m / f)	*cousin*
prioridade (f)	*priority*
pro / pra (= para o / a)	*for the*
procura	*search;* **à procura de** *looking for / on the lookout for*
produtos (m pl) **de limpeza**	*cleaning products*
professor(ora) (m / f)	*teacher*
proibido fumar	*no smoking*
promoção (f)	*promotion* (sale); **em promoção** *on special offer*
pronto!	*there!*
provador (m)	*changing room*
provar	*to try*
próximo(a)	*next*

qual?	*what / which?*
quantos? / quantas? (m pl / fpl)	*how many?*
quarta-feira (f)	*Wednesday*
quarteirão (m)	*block (street)*
quarto (m)	*(bed)room*
quarto (m) **de casal**	*double room*
quarto (m) **de solteiro**	*single room*
quarto (m) **para família**	*family room*
quarto(a)	*fourth*
quase nunca	*almost never / hardly ever*
que	*that / which / who*
que lindo(a)	*how pretty / lovely!*
que sorte!	*what good luck!*
que tal ...?	*how about / what about ...?*
queijo (m)	*cheese*
quente	*hot*
querer	*to want / wish*
quinta-feira (f)	*Thursday*
quinto(a)	*fifth*
rádio (m)	*radio*
rapidinho	*really quick*
raramente	*rarely*
razão (f)	*reason*
real (m) (pl **reais**)	*Real (currency)*
realmente	*really*
receita (f)	*recipe*
recepção (f)	*reception*
recepcionista (m / f)	*receptionist*
recheado(a)	*filled / stuffed*
recomendar	*to recommend*
rede social (f)	*social media network*
refeição (pl **refeições**) (f)	*meal*
refeição (f) **rápida**	*light meal*
relaxante	*relaxing*
relaxar	*to relax*
relógio (m)	*clock / watch*
repetir	*to repeat*
reportagem (f)	*news broadcast*
reserva (f)	*reservation / (nature) reserve*

responder *to reply*
restaurante (m) *restaurant*
reunião (f) *meeting*
Reveillon (m) *New Year's Eve*
rio (m) *river*
ritmo (m) *rhythm*
rodeado(a) por *surrounded by*
rodoviária (f) *bus station*
rosa (f) *rose / pink*
roupas (f pl) *clothes*
roxo(a) *purple*
rua (f) *street / road*
ruim *awful*
ruivo(a) *red-haired*
sábado (m) *Saturday*
saber *to know (a fact / how to do something)*
saia (f) *skirt*
saída (f) **de emergência** *emergency exit*
sair *to go out*
sal (m) *salt*
sala (f) **(de reuniões)** *(meeting) room*
salada (f) *salad*
saladinha (f) *small salad*
salão (m) **de festa** *party room*
salgado(a) *salty*
sandálias (f pl) *sandals*
sanduíche (m) *sandwich*
sapatos (m pl) *shoes*
saudade (f) *feeling of missing someone or something*
saúde (f) *health*
saúde! *cheers!*
secretário(a) (m / f) *secretary*
seda (f) *silk*
seguir *to follow / carry on*
segunda-feira (f) *Monday*
segundo(a) *second*
senha (f) *password*
selva (f) *jungle*
semana (f) *week*

semana passada (f)	*last week*
Semana Santa (f)	*Holy Week*
sempre	*always*
sentir-se	*to feel*
separado(a)	*separated*
ser	*to be*
servir (-se)	*to serve (yourself)*
sétimo(a)	*seventh*
seu/s (m / pl)	*his / her / its / your*
sexta-feira (f)	*Friday*
sexto(a)	*sixth*
shopping (m)	*shopping center*
short (m)	*shorts*
show (m) **de música**	*music show*
sim	*yes*
sinal (m) **de trânsito**	*traffic lights*
sinceramente	*sincerely / truthfully*
só	*only / just*
sobre	*about*
sobremesa (f)	*dessert*
sobrenome (m)	*surname*
sobrinho(a) (m / f)	*nephew / niece*
sogro (m), **sogra** (f)	*father / mother in law*
solteiro(a)	*single*
som (pl **sons**) (m)	*sound*
sombra (f)	*shade;* **na sombra** *in the shade*
sorvete (m)	*ice cream*
sua/s (f / pl)	*his / her / its / your*
subir	*to go up / climb*
subsolo (m)**: no subsolo**	*underground*
suco (m)	*juice*
sueco(a)	*Swedish*
sugerir	*to suggest*
sujo(a)	*dirty*
sunga (f)	*swimming trunks*
supermercado (m)	*supermarket*
suportar	*to put up with*
surpreender-se	*to surprise oneself*
tá?	*OK?*

talvez	*perhaps*
tamanho (m)	*size*
tão	*so*
tarde	*afternoon / evening;* **da / de tarde** *in the afternoon / evening*
tchau	*bye*
tchin tchin!	*cheers!*
teatro (m)	*theatre*
tecido (m)	*fabric*
técnico(a) de Informática	*IT technician*
telefonar	*to phone*
tempão (m)	*long time*
tempo (m)	*weather / time*
tênis (m / m pl)	*tennis / trainers*
ter	*to have*
ter jeito	*to work out / be convenient*
terça-feira (f)	*Tuesday*
terceiro(a)	*third*
terminar	*to end / finish*
terno (m)	*suit*
tio(a) (m / f)	*uncle / aunt*
tipo (m)	*type / sort*
tirar	*to take / take out*
tô (= estou)	*I'm*
toalha (f)	*towel*
tocar	*to touch / play (instrument)*
tomar	*to have (drink) / take (medicine)*
torneira (f)	*tap*
torrada (f)	*toast*
trabalhar	*to work*
trabalho (m)	*work*
tranquilo(a)	*calm*
travesseiro (m)	*pillow*
trazer	*to bring*
trem (pl **trens**) (m)	*train*
trilha (f)	*trail*
triste	*sad*
troco (m)	*change (money)*
turismo (m) **de aventura**	*adventure tourism*

último(a)	*last*
um pouco	*a little (bit)*
universidade (f)	*university*
usar	*to use / wear*
uso (m) **exclusivo**	*exclusive use*
vale a pena	*it's worth it*
valeu!	*good stuff! / you bet! / appreciated! / thanks!*
variedade (f)	*variety*
vatapá (m)	*shrimp curry*
vegano(a)	*vegan*
vegetariano(a)	*vegetarian*
veludo (m)	*velvet*
vender	*to sell*
ventilador (m)	*fan*
ver	*to see*
verão (m)	*summer*
verdade!	*true! / correct!*
verde	*green*
vermelho(a)	*red*
vestido (m)	*dress*
vestir-se	*to get dressed*
vez (f)	*time;* **uma vez** *once*
viagem (pl **viagens**) (f)	*journey*
viajar	*to travel*
vinagre (m)	*vinegar*
vinho (m)	*wine*
vinho (m) **da casa**	*house wine*
vinho (m) **tinto / branco**	*red / white wine*
vir	*to come*
virar	*to turn*
visita (f)	*visit*
visitante (m)	*visitor*
visitar	*to visit*
vista (f)	*view;* **à vista** *in cash / debit*
vitrine (f)	*shop window*
viúvo(a) (m / f)	*widower / widow*
vivo (ao vivo)	*live (performance)*
vizinhos (m pl)	*neighbours*

você/s	*you*
vôlei (m)	*volleyball*
voltar	*to return*
vontade	*will;* **à vontade** *at will*
voo (m)	*flight*
xadrez (m)	*chess*
x-búrguer (m)	*cheeseburger*
xícara (f) **de café**	*cup of coffee*
xinxim (m) **de galinha**	*spicy chicken stew*

Can-do statements

UNIT	CEFR level	ACTFL level	CAN-DO STATEMENTS
UNIT 1	**A1**	**Novice High**	I can establish basic social contact by using the simplest everyday polite forms of: greetings and farewells; introductions. I can ask and answer questions about myself and other people.
UNIT 2	**A1 / A2**	**Novice High / Intermediate Low**	I can handle numbers. (A1) I can ask and answer questions about myself and other people. (A1) I can describe my family. (A2)
UNIT 3	**A1 / A2**	**Novice High / Intermediate Low**	I can recognize familiar names, words and very basic phrases on simple notices (menus). (A1) I can say what I like/dislike. (A2) I can order a meal. (A2)
UNIT 4	**A1 / A2**	**Novice High / Intermediate Low**	I can reply in an interview to simple direct questions. (A1) I can describe habits and routine. I can ask and answer questions about habits and routines.
UNIT 5	**A1 / A2**	**Novice High / Intermediate Low**	I can handle numbers, cost and time. (A1) I can get simple information about travel, use public transport and buy tickets. (A2) I can find specific, predictable information in simple everyday material such as timetables. (A2)
UNIT 6	**A1 / A2**	**Novice High / Intermediate Low**	I can understand instructions addressed carefully and slowly, and follow short, simple directions (written or spoken). (A1) I can ask very simply for repetition when I do not understand. (A2) I can ask for and give directions referring to a map or a plan. (A2)

UNIT 7	**A1 / A2**	**Novice High / Intermediate Low**	I can pass on personal details in written form. (A1) I can deal with common aspects of everyday living such as lodgings. (A2) I can for and provide personal information. (A2)
UNIT 8	**A1 / A2**	**Novice High / Intermediate Low**	I can ask people for things. (A1) I can handle numbers and quantities. (A1) I can make simple purchases by stating what is wanted and asking the price. (A2)
UNIT 9	**A2**	**Intermediate Low**	I can describe plans and arrangements. I can make and respond to invitations, suggestions and apologies. I can understand short, simple personal letters or messages.
UNIT 10	**A1**	**Intermediate Low**	I can ask and answer questions about pastimes. I can describe past activities and personal experiences.. I can explain what I like or dislike about something.